FEAR THE 4ᵀᴴ ANGEL

HE WHO ASSIST GOD

Aliym

Book and Cover design by Spirit Pixels
ISBN-13:9780692890165

First Edition: May 2017

10 9 8 7 6 5 4 3 2 1

CONTENTS

PREFACE

Are you happy with the world you live in today? Do you feel safe? Do you trust people? Do you think of yourself as a kind and caring person? Are you suspicious of people who don't look like you? Do you feel rage at the slightest inconvenience? Do you feel that you could take the life of another human being? If you answered no to the first part of this paragraph and yes to the last part, then this book is for you.

This book was written for those who believe in a higher power and who believe that we may have to answer to the spiritual beings who monitor humanity's deeds and thoughts. As the fabric of the entire world seems to be crumbling, this book was written for those who are contributing to the deterioration and devaluation of life on all levels: the wars, the poverty, the pillaging of nations, the raping of women, the discarding of infants, the greed of those who already have more than enough, and the 'why?' questions of those who have nothing.

This is our world. So, is God watching? Do the spirit beings care? Do they even exist? If they do, then why is life so terrible at times? This book is for those who ask these questions. How do you get through life? Do you ignore your conscience when it speaks to you . . . when at certain times it urges you not to be negative? Does the sound of your inner voice resonate in your heart and mind and you wish it would go away, or do you listen intently and make the right choices?

Today, many of us behave as if we have no conscience, no feelings, and no guilt. We easily hurt other human beings, easily hurt animals in the wild, and destroy our environment by decimating our forests and poisoning our water and air.

Based on the way in which human beings behave, it seems we would like to trade places with four-footed creatures. What we're forgetting is that the four-footed so-called beasts only kill for food or to protect themselves from the supposedly more evolved animal—man. Based on human beings' insensitive behavior and the hardening of our hearts, which is leading to the deterioration of life on this planet, it appears things are becoming less shocking every day.

Are we becoming accustomed to our own destructive ways? Are we desensitized to the point that when we hear about the most horrific crimes, we merely take a moment to hope that a similar tragedy doesn't befall us, our families, or even our possessions, and then we return to our daily routines? Many of us ask, If God exists, why does he or she allow such terrible things to happen?

Well, imagine if I gave you a beautiful house on spacious land with well-manicured lawns, rosebushes, and fruit trees on the premises. I then said to you, "I'll come back to visit you in two years to see how you've progressed. This house is yours, so take care of it." Two years later, I returned only to find the yard no longer manicured, the rosebushes overgrown and thorny, the fruit trees chopped down, and the foundation of the house crumbling. Would you ask why I let this terrible thing happen to you and your house?

So, is God angry at humanity, or is humanity angry with God? Who has the right to be angry at the other? Is it the one who gave everything and asked only that we take care of all that was given and of each other? Or is it the one who acts selfishly, monstrously, and who will stop at nothing to obtain more of everything? If God is angry, the anger toward us would be justified. I believe we are like the children who behave in an unruly manner throughout their youth and then become angry at their parents because they turn out to be a disappointment. We live in a world of rebellion—nation rebelling against nation and all people rebelling against each other. Nature is also rebelling; she is sick and is cleansing herself of human beings. Tornadoes, hurricanes, tsunamis, earthquakes, and even the four-footed creatures are rebelling. They used to fear and avoid contact with human beings; now they have become the aggressors.

Are we in the last days? Well, the holy books say yes, we are. Those books warn of these signs of the time and tell us we should guard against evil, protect our virtue, be kind to each other, be kind to creatures, and, most of all, remember God. The day will come when we will all leave this world for the next one, stand before the Great Spirit being, and answer for and be judged according to our deeds, which will be weighed. However you perceive it to be, the most high will call us back.

Many believe that Heaven is a place where only great things will be presented to you if you're fortunate enough to have God accept you there. But what if it isn't that way at all? What if Heaven is your own personal space somewhere in the afterlife and you still have to prove yourself worthy of being there even after you've made it to that realm?

The question is, have you given thought to what happens after you die? Do you believe in life after death? Do you believe that you may stand before a committee of spiritual beings who will question you about your journey in this realm? Will you be ready? Will your good deeds outweigh your bad ones? Or will you be like the man in this story, twenty-eight-year-old Jonathan Krause, who lives for himself and lives only for today? Krause is a prominent man with a slight appetite for drugs, sex, and money. On the surface, he seems to have the life most young men want. He lives in a fast-paced big city, owns a spacious apartment, and has a great job, a beautiful girlfriend, and enough money to support the fun he likes to have.

But he is a man with a deep-seeded past, and although his troubles began in his youth, he has never given real thought to any of the questionable decisions he made back then. He has suppressed these memories or has simply never spoken about them. Spirituality was never something he reflected on because, to him, it was not real. In fact, it was just plain stupid, and he never felt the need to adhere to his inner self as far as feeding his soul and spirit was concerned. He lived and did as he pleased regardless of the effects of his actions.

But Jonathan Krause will soon have to face all his suppressions of the past, all his carelessness in the present, and all his denial of the future. The angel is coming for him and will return him to the Most High God. He will meet, talk to, and even become angry with this young man. Yes, even before his physical death, Jonathan Krause will meet the angel of death. This meeting will be an inquiry into Jonathan's past, present, and future, and it will take place over a ten-day period, which is all the time he has left to live. This young man will challenge, verbally abuse, and even attempt to physically harm the angel. With insolence buried deep in his heart and mind, he will stoke the wrath of this Supreme Being. And for Jonathan's provocation, the angel will force him to acknowledge things he has refused to acknowledge with regard to spirituality. He will show Jonathan the supernatural, ignore his pleas for more time on earth, taunt him, frighten him, and bring him to his knees. And all this will be done so that he might purge himself before being taken from this realm into the spirit world, where life will take on a whole new meaning.

CHAPTER 1
YAADILAHI THE SCRIBE

My name is Yaadilahi [The hand of God], and, as all spiritual beings, I was born after the order of the great four, and the son of two lesser spirit beings, these two spirit beings made the decision to leave the spiritual realm and become physical beings. For their decision, I was left to be a child of paradise, existing on the closest realm of the Most High. There is no better place than this, except to live where our Creator dwells and no spirit can exist there, for this realm is full of an inconceivable power where only the four can approach.

As I grew in understanding of the levels of existence, I also was given the choice of becoming a physical being, but, being shown in the spirit world, what the physical being would endure in these realms, I made the decision to remain an ethereal being.

My existence has, and will always be, one of learning and progression toward our Creator. And, for this, I've been chosen to be a student of the great four, to learn from each one, as they are the best of teachers. These four are taught by the one that has not been taught by any but is the knower of all things. These four have given to me what they call limited knowledge, and, even with this, I still feel I am filled with knowledge. I have been shown or called to hear some of the events the four bring into existence by the commands of the Supreme Creator. And, as not to eliminate even the slightest details when giving an account of my experience to my brothers and sisters in this realm; I've become a great scribe.

I am the writer of all I see and have not seen, for these four who I consider my parents have spoken to me the ways of our Creator. They have shown me the gifts bestowed on them by our Creator. So, the quill has become a part of my limb, for my words are not my words but all that I see and hear by way of my teachers. And, as they cross from one dimension to the next I cross with them, quill in hand, taking account.

I've been to many realms of existence, each time with at least one of the four; sometimes two of the teachers and sometimes all four will I accompany to the physical realms at the same time. I often travel there with Gibrael, the [news bearer], as witness to his interaction with all the prophets, and he is adamant that a scribe be present when he visits the lower realms, for he is a perfectionist at teaching men and those that are not men what our Creator teaches him. And, during my travels with him, I am commanded by this great being to make a record.

He says to me, "Write all that I say and do, for neither my words, nor my action will be denied at a later time." His meaning is that no life form will bare false witness against him as to what he did or did not teach or what he did or did not accomplish. Their allegiance to the Creator is above all things, and they do not disappoint the Creator.

My other exhibitions were with the leader of the four, Miykael, and at my first encounter with him, so amazed was I at his ability, I felt that I should fall down at his feet and worship him. He interrupted my thoughts and asked, "Are you not from the upper realm?" His voice was subtle but powerful, like the sound of many stringed musical instruments. I lowered my head and dared not look at him, I immediately knew my transgression, and I answered.

"Indeed, I am, majestic one."

"Then surely you are aware that all praise is for the one that produced even me and all that come after me." He replied.

I immediately sought forgiveness from our Creator with prayer, and instantly my guilt left me. But this being Miykael, he did not appear as an imposing being, and this was done by design, so as not to intimidate those blessed to be in his presence. For he is an immensely powerful spiritual being, to be discussed in detail later.

This day the soul collector, also known as Azraa'el, appeared to me in a physical form, standing twelve feet in height, looking very stern. His eyes were dark and piercing. And although he existed forever with the Most High, he appeared ageless. His hair was black with silver streaks, and it outlined his face and fell past his shoulders and down his back. His garment was a white jallabiya and a lengthy white cloak worn on his shoulders. He spoke with the voice of a hollowed mountain, and commanded me saying, "Yaadilahi, come out from your ethereal form."

I moved closer, kneeled before him, and replied, "My Lord, I cannot."

Confused he responded, "What prevents you from presenting yourself? We're you not taught by Miykael and Gibrael, my brothers, how to present yourself in the physical form?"

"No, my Lord, I have not been taught."

He then put forth his hand and removed my ethereal force, and I became a physical being.

He said to me, "Since it is that you have traveled with Miykael and Gibrael first, and they have not shown you how to transfigure, then neither will I. Now go scribe, take up your quill and accompany me to the lowest realm where the physical beings dwell and write all that I show you, and write all that I speak to you."

I took hold of his arm and moved throughout the universe, and this seemed to be the simplest of tasks. We crossed dimensions and realms and were greeted with reverence in all realms, from the smallest to the greatest levels of life. And, he communicated with even the most insignificant of creatures, and entertained their discussions of life in their realm.

The inhabitants of these realms loved him; I loved him, and I wished for a minute portion of his essence. He would interrupt my thoughts each time I thought to worship him saying, "There is none like the one who created even me." He would say with a warm smile. Knowing I was a mere child, as far as attaining his level of spiritual knowledge, he was ever tolerant of me. He lifted me with confidence and he instructed me that I should be mindful of all things, of all beings, of all life, from the highest forms to the lowest forms.

This is a trait of our Creator, and what our Creator does so shall we do. These four beings are of the highest intelligence, and crossing dimensions and existing on the many different levels of life are but a simple thought for them. This is not a thing I would attempt alone, mastery of the highest levels of science and knowledge of all the realms of existence must be used. Although I have traveled to the lower realms, I am not so confidant or skilled in the science of traveling into other dimensions alone.

So I will join Azraa'el in realm traveling again, as a student and a scribe. For the soul he is to retrieve is the vessel for an even greater soul and the soul that will come is the potential for moving the human being forward.

I will speak to you of many events, some of which occurred before my existence, some of these I did witness, and some have been spoken to me; I am the scribe Yaadilahi, today I follow Azraa'el and this is the story."

CHAPTER 2

THE CALL

After the beginning, after the Most High completed the physical aspects of creation, and the spiritual beings were brought into existence, and, after the landscaping of the universe was complete and the war between the sons and daughters of GOD had ended, order was restored on the spiritual realm. Peace was the way of existence for two eons. Soon after, the Most High caused the evolution of man, and brought him to a position of prominence. Then the Supreme Being called the four.

"MIYKAEL ...GIBRAEL ...RAPHAEL ...AZRAA'EL ..., ascend to the highest realm."

The angelic beings moved toward the Most High with great speed, appearing as light. They then transformed into men and stood before their Creator. The realm of the Most High was brilliant; an explosion of colors went on continuously and magnified its presence.

The four beings shielded themselves from the powerful aura of the Most High, and, fearing their disintegration from the light, each one took the feathers of the colored peacock and made them to cover their entire bodies from head to foot. The colors of this bird are the same colors that surround the Most High's realm.

The Supreme Being spoke with the four beings. "You four are my spiritual leaders, I consider you my offspring and I am well pleased with you all. Miykael, you have defeated Iblis, the rebellious one, and cast down him and his two-hundred fallen soldiers, who were also

9

considered my offspring. For your will, your truth in spirit, and for being the first to bring justice to those who have made the decision to be rebellious, you will be my first in command. Your power will be unlimited; none will overcome you; your strength and power will be unmatched. From this moment forward, knowledge of all things is given to you, the inner workings, the science of how I bring into existence whatever situation I please, I pass on to you. This knowledge is called the science of life, and you should remember me for I have bestowed upon you this great knowledge and none will surpass you. Access to every portal throughout the universe is granted to you, and these spiritual beings I have called will stand beside you, but nothing and no one will be above you, none but me, and, from now until I call you back, you will be known as Miykael the one who is most like the Most High."

Miykael was grateful to the Creator. "Thank you my Lord, I receive this blessing and will forever be your grateful servant. As for those who became rebellious, their attempts to take control of the universe without your permission we saw as a great offense, so we took great pleasure in removing them from your presence. And they were defeated by the power given to me by you, and I am grateful, oh Supreme One, I humbly accept my position, and my allegiance is to you forever."

The Creator spoke to Gibrael. "Gibrael, For following Miykael into battle against those who rebelled, and for assisting in their expulsion, and for a constant yearning to communicate with me and learning the ways of spirituality, I charge you with bringing my message to all beings. From this moment on, access to the mind of all beings throughout the universe is given to you. You will appear on all realms of existence, taking on the shape and likeness of those inhabitants of that realm, and you will remind them of their spirituality and of how they should work to perfect it. You may convey our message however you determine, you will use subtlety, and you will be their subconscious. Because you penetrate their minds, some will adapt and learn the spiritual gift of prophesying and knowing what is hidden. These will be the prophets of that realm. You will appear when they call out for us to assist them, and you may penetrate their sleep and enter their dreams. You will communicate all I have taught you and you are my second in command, and you will follow your brother Miykael in power and rank. From now until I call you back, you will be known as Gibrael the revealer."

Gibrael was grateful to the Creator. "Thank you my Lord, I receive this blessing and will forever be a grateful servant. As for those who rebelled, we took great pleasure in casting out those who disobeyed your command and sought power without your blessing. As you have revealed to me the mysteries of the spirit world, I, by your command, will reveal to the lesser beings, those things which they do not know. I am grateful, Oh Supreme One, and I humbly accept my position. My allegiance is to you forever."

The Creator spoke to Raphael. "Raphael, for following Miykael and Gibrael into battle, and for destroying many of the rebels with a blast of the shofar, by my command, you will sound this instrument in our spiritual realm to signal anytime a great event is to occur in any of the physical realms.

You will teach all the lesser beings the sound of melody, they will enjoy this sound, and you will inspire some of these beings with this artful noise. When the beings hear your joyous noise, it will be accepted, and they will call this sound music.

You will create instruments of all kinds to make the sounds of music, and some of these beings will learn these instruments and will bring about this music from within. And, they will excel in making the art of noise, but none will surpass you in the knowledge of these instruments, and, when the beings hear music, it will bring them joy, and this sound will affect every living thing throughout the universe. The art of noise is a creation of your Lord, and you will bring this creation to all the levels of existence, and, because the shofar was the first instrument to be sounded in the spiritual realm, you will use it to carry frequencies. These frequencies will be used to destroy those who seek to destroy, and you will raise all beings from their physical death on the last day with these frequencies. You will be my third in command and you will follow Gibrael in power and in rank, and, from now until I call you back, you will be known as Raphael the noise maker."

Raphael was grateful to the Most High. "Thank you my Lord, I receive this blessing and will forever be a grateful servant. As for those rebellious ones who chose to go astray, we took great pleasure in putting them out. For blessing me with the shofar, I will craft instruments with my own hands, I will give each instrument its own sound, and I will make beautiful melodies. These melodies will be for the pleasure of my Creator, for blessing me with the art of noise. I, by your command, will inspire certain beings to possess this ability before leaving the spirit realm for the physical world. At their physical birth, they will hear the art of noise sounding in heaven, and, from then on, they will possess the ability to produce the sound called music on that realm. I am grateful, oh Supreme One, and I humbly accept my position; my allegiance is to you forever."

The Creator spoke to Azraa'el. "Azraa'el, for following Miykael, Gibrael and Raphael into battle against the ones who chose to rebel, and for grabbing hold of the soul of one of the rebels, as he did die a physical and spiritual death while in battle with the righteous.

You will inform all beings throughout the universe that their last breaths are with the Most High. You will inform them that there is no more sustenance on any level of existence and that when their predetermined time is up, their physical body will fail them, and their soul will return to the All Powerful.

You will travel to all levels to retrieve these souls and you will command an army of a great number. As I have created them to live forever. The man will be deceived and bring about his own physical death. He will first experience the physical death, and if he does not wish not to continue in the spirit then eventually that will also die. Although the lower beings will pray not to return to me, and even when you have compassion on them in their time of despair, you will inform them you are not able to prevent the inevitable and you will show compassion and remove their souls with patience. There are some to whom you will not wish to show compassion and you will approach them, however you determine, but be careful never to cause the spiritual death of any being, that is a choice left to them. You will be my fourth in command, and you will follow Raphael in power and rank. You will be known as the soul collector in the spirit world, but, in the physical, you will unfairly be called the angel of death.

Azraa'el's demeanor became full of sadness. "O Merciful One, I took great pleasure in defeating the outcasts who wished to attain power through deception, rebelling against your orders to revere man as the appointed leader in the physical realm. I question not your judgment, but I plead with you, charge me not with this assignment, I worry man will hate me unjustly; all creation will despise me for that matter. I will be looked upon as a curse; for I will bring nothing but death when I appear to them, and they will not comprehend that, before their physical existence, the giver of life decided their time. They will associate your servant with nothing good; rather, they will associate me with death and destruction."

The Most High responded. "No Azraa'el, the lower beings will be too involved with themselves and the trials of life. Their journey will be a difficult one if they turn against the spiritual. You will not be thought of, except when the time is approaching for their return. Now go forth all of you and be mindful that you are spiritual beings. And you should protect your spirituality with great diligence and know for certain that I will call all creation back and your return is to me."

The four beings departed from the highest realm. Azraa'el and a legion of spirit beings to assist Him descended to the physical realm in an instant. This is the story told to me, Yaadilahi, by the great four.

CHAPTER 3
THE FIRST MEETING

The angel appeared in the city of New York in the year 2000 on a Tuesday at 11:30am, as the sun shined brightly against the beautiful blue sky. Azraa'el positioned himself in the heart of the city and walked among the people. The sound of the place was vibrant. As he walked the streets, he glanced at many and knew their fate, but they gave him no thought, and neither could they perceive their approaching end. I addressed my lord and teacher that we should warn them of what was to come, and instantly, without him speaking a word, I knew that these would meet their own personal soul collector shortly.

After walking four miles he stopped and stood on the corner of an intersecting street, he looked east then west and crossed to the opposite side. He continued walking a short distance then stood across the street from a warehouse turned into an apartment building, and waited.

Azraa'el sat down on the curb of the street and watched for two hours, as people came and went, in and out of the building. He saw a young man in his mid to late twenties come out of the building and focused his attention on him.

The man was striking in appearance; he stood six feet in height, had dusty brown hair and was clean-shaven. He wore a long coat

14

over his clothing, a dark-blue suit, a white collared shirt, and a dark-blue tie; his shoes matched the color of his hair, and he looked to be in need of nothing.

As he moved, Azraa'el moved with him, and then I knew that this was the man we had come for. As he walked he passed by one who was in dire need and this one put forth his hand and asked,

"Can you spare some change?"

Our subject ignored the needy soul and continued walking, waving and smiling hello to people in the neighborhood. He stopped at a stand and bought a newspaper and mints, then continued to the next intersection. He raised his hand in the air, attempting to stop a car to get him to his place of business. And, with this Azraa'el removed our physical form, and we were spirit again, sitting next to the man in the car.

I looked at him closely, he smelled of a beautiful scent. His garments were of the finest quality, and on his lap sat a carrying case trimmed with gold. He tapped on it with his fingers, while looking out the window of the car as we moved quickly to his destination. He fumbled around for something, patting his chest, patting his pockets, lifting himself off his seat and going through the inner pocket of his coat. He pulled out his telephone and spoke.

"Hello, yes I'm on my way, I'll be there in a few minutes, hey buddy can you step on it?"

The driver of the vehicle responded by accelerating. We moved faster, and as I sat looking at this man with a bit of admiration. Azraa'el also stared at him but with not so much admiration. His was a look of stern concentration.

He spoke to me mentally saying, "I see you are over taken by the dress and outer appearance of this man, be mindful O scribe, never accept the outer layers of any being, for the outer layer is not who they are. For we judge by spirit, heart, and soul, and again the soul is judged many more times, for it belongs to the Creator of all things. And so my gazing into this man's eyes and into his chest allows me to review his life, for when I stand before him in the physical there will be no denying the facts concerning him."

15

I nodded in agreement with the soul collector, and we continued evaluating this man as he sorted through papers still in his carrying case. We arrived at the destination. The man paid the driver and exited the car; we stayed a few feet behind him as we followed.

The man hurried into a large building, acknowledging the security guards as he walked past them toward a set of elevators. He paced impatiently as he waited, checking his watch and looking up at the numbers indicating the floors that the elevators were on.

Azraa'el stood against the wall with his arms folded and watched the man–5 ...4 ...3 ...2 ...1, the doors open. He quickly boarded and pressed for the twenty-fifth floor. Before the doors closed, a beautiful woman boarded the elevator. She looked at him warmly; he smiled at her. She turned her back to him and pressed the button for the thirty-fifth floor. He bit his hand, silently expressing his thoughts about her physical appearance. Azraa'el stared at the man. The doors closed, and we went up.

The young man exited the elevator, but not before saying to the woman, "You have a nice day now."

"You have a good day also." She replied.

He walked through a small corridor and through a set of doors, and then ran a card into a box that gave him access to a room where a hundred other people, speaking loudly, sat at desks and tables. The telephones, the computers, there was much commotion in this room.

As he walked to his desk, someone yelled from across the room at him.

"Hey Jonathan, what's up buddy? You're late."

He threw his hands up in a carefree manner and replied. "New York city traffic what do you want me to do?"

"Well I don't know about the traffic situation but I could use your help with something." The man walked over

Jonathan looked at this man with a smirk and asked, "What is it now Todd?"

"Uh I need a small loan."

"Awe, come on man, I loaned you money two months ago, You still haven't paid me back. How much is it this time?"

"I know, I know you've been there for me, and I'm gonna pay you back. I just got a little behind on some of my bills. You know how it is."

Annoyed, Jonathan flopped down in his chair and leaned back. "No I really don't know how it is."

"Ok This is the last time. Come on man, It's not like it's gonna break you."

"How much are we talking?"

"All I need is three-thousand dollars."

"Three-thousand dollars, what the hell, Todd! See I know what your problem is, you're getting in over your head with that shit."

"Oh, like you don't indulge."

"Yes, I indulge a little, but not to the point where it takes over my life and I start acting irresponsible."

"Shit Jonathan, if I wanted a lecture, I'd have gone to my parents, you gonna help me out or what?"

"Hey don't give me that attitude; you have to cut this stuff out or you're going to end up losing everything. I'm telling you this as a friend." Todd shook his head in a disagreeing manner, as if frustrated by the friendly advice.

"Ok I hear you, so you're gonna help me out, right?"

"Yeah, I'll help you, but this is it, no more."

"Hey thanks man. I really appreciate it, and just so you know, it's not all spent on drugs."

"Yeah, whatever, I'll write you a check, don't blow it."

"I won't and thanks again."

A few hours had passed. Azraa'el sat in front of Jonathan watching 'his every move, listening to his thoughts, reviewing in his mind the entire life of this man, and waiting for the time to retrieve his soul.

"So what are you doing tonight, Johnny boy?" Todd asked.

"I don't know, nothing really, why?"

"See that guy over there?"

"Yeah, what about him?"

"He's the new VP for the accounting departments, doesn't look much older than us and already calling the shots."

"Somebody here must really like him, huh?" Jonathan replied

"That's not all; he has these wild parties at his place in the Hamptons."

"The Hamptons?"

"Yeah, and listen, he's got a Rolls, a Ferrari, a Lamborghini, an Olympic-size swimming pool, horses, the whole nine yards and all of it sitting on seventeen acres. I hear he does a mountain of the good stuff too." [Todd pointing to his nose]

"What'd he do, marry the bosses daughter?"

"I told you he's the vice president for accounting."

"I know VP's make a lot here, but that much?"

"Oh no, my friend, you're mistaking him for being vice president just for here, oh no, he's vice president here, the Midwest offices, the west coast offices, and the overseas office."

Jonathan looked surprised and he stared at the sharply dressed slightly graying young man. "Damn, he can't be more than forty, he's gotta know somebody high up."

"I don't know, but I tell you what I do know, he's having one of his famous parties tonight, and we need to be there."

"Were stock brokers Todd, they're presidents, vice presidents, 'CEO's, you know how they are at times, were cool for the yearly office Christmas party, the annual company picnic, but to go to one of their houses for a social gathering, when does that ever happen?"

"No, see that's the thing, from what I hear, the guy is a total party animal, sure, here in the office, he's suit, tie, and all business, but once he's out of the office bam! He turns into a freaking rock star. Come on we gotta go, Jonathan."

"I don't know, I think I told Steph we were gonna hang tonight."

"Well did you tell her, or didn't you?"

"I don't remember, today's Friday, but I don't know if I said Friday or Saturday. I better call her and ask."

"No, no, no, if you call her and ask she'll definitely make you hang with her tonight. What you do is, not call, go to the party tonight, and if anything, you'll see her tomorrow."

"I don't know I feel like I'm doing something wrong, I just got out of the dog house with her from standing her up on that couples date she had planned for us a few weeks back. I don't wanna mess up with her again over some dumb party."

"Look, you said you weren't sure if you were seeing her tonight, has she called to confirm anything?"

"No, not yet."

"Well see, there you go, women call all day long when you're supposed to do something with them. We'll give her a couple more hours to call, and if she doesn't call you by then, then you know you don't have a date with her. She'd probably rather be with her girlfriends tonight anyway, cause God knows, you're not hitting that right."

"Yeah right." Jonathan said sarcastically.

"Ok, I'll wait until five. She calls, I'm not going to the party, she doesn't call, I'll go, simple as that."

"Fair enough. Hey, this could be good for our careers here, hob knob with some power players and make some connections."

"Yeah, sure, good for our career, and deadly for my relationship."

"Hey, Jonathan?"

"What?"

"Can you do me one more favor?"

"What do you want now?"

"PLEASE GROW A PAIR!"

Jonathan nodded his head in agreement, and then showed Todd his middle finger. Both men laughed. Todd began walking back to his cubicle on the other side of the room, and then Jonathan stood up from his chair and shouted to Todd.

"Hey what are you doing for lunch?"

"What do you feel like?" Todd replied.

"I could go for some Chinese, the place on Fifty-Sixth Street."

"Yeah, that sounds good." Jonathan sat back in his chair and, for an hour, made phone calls, shuffled through papers, and frantically tapped the key board of his computer. He looked at the clock; it was one o'clock. "Lunch time," he said, as he rose from his chair. He grabbed his overcoat and walked toward Todd.

"Hey you ready?"

"Yes."

As the two men walked toward the door of the large office room, Azraa'el walked out in front of them, then turned and stared into the eyes of Todd and reviewed his life. Then he walked toward the elevators and waited.

"Hey man, I can't wait until tonight, booze, food, and hot, scantily clad women everywhere, I'm sure of it!" Todd said with joyful anticipation.

"Don't count me in for this just yet, Todd. I told you, if she calls, I'm not going. But speaking of hot, on my way up this morning, this really hot blonde got on the elevator with me, she was gorgeous I wonder what company she's with."

"Well don't worry about that because we'll have plenty to choose from later tonight my friend."

"Hey, if I go to this party, and right now that's a big if, I'm not going there to hook up with anybody, and listen to you, what about Emily, don't you care about her?"

"Of course I care about her but, like the saying goes, what they don't know doesn't hurt." Todd said with a devilish grin.

"Yeah well I love Stephanie, and I can't afford to get caught doing something stupid, so don't expect me to get wild and crazy."

"Awe man, what happen to you, when did you turn into this gigantic wuss? ... Jesus!"

"I'm just saying, I'm gonna play it cool, and you should do the same, don't get to crazy at the bosses house, you get too loose, and it always comes back to bite you in the ass."

"Ok, Mr. Rogers, let's go. The elevator's here."

As the doors were closing, a man screamed out. "Hold it!" "Hey, Jonathan, Todd."

"What's up, Tim?"

"You guys didn't forget about Sunday, did you?" Both Todd and Jonathan looked puzzled.

"What's Sunday?" Todd asked.

"The charity for the kid's. Come on guys, you remember we discussed this about a month ago. You said you would come down and give us a hand raising money."

"Oh Yeah, we'll be there Tim, you can count on us. Right, Todd?" Jonathan said.

"Absolutely, we'll be there for sure."

"Ok guy's, great, see you Sunday at one o'clock." Tim waved good-bye to Todd and Jonathan as he got off the elevator.

"Perfect, roped into a charity event." Todd griped.

"Stop bitching. This is for a good cause helping kids, you know. There's nothing wrong with helping out once in a while."

"Since when did you become so philanthropic, freaking Gandhi over here?"

"When did I become so philanthropic, how about three hours ago when you asked me for three-thousand dollars, that's when?"

"Whatever." Todd replied.

The two men walked out of the building. Azraa'el followed for a short distance, then transported himself to the restaurant before them, and sat at the table the two friends would eat at. After five minutes and four city blocks, the subject and his friend entered the restaurant.

The manager greeted them. "How many will there be sir?" He asked Jonathan.

"Just the two of us." Jonathan replied.

"Ok, right this way gentleman." The manager led Jonathan and Todd to what appeared to be an unoccupied table, they sat down across from one another. Jonathan unknowingly sat next to Azraa'el.

A waiter quickly approached. "Something to drink, gentleman?"

"Yes, I'll have a Sprite and a glass of water."

"I will have a vodka double, on the rocks."

"What are you crazy Todd? You're gonna go back to work drunk, What's with the liquid lunch?"

"What are you, my wet nurse? I'm just taking the edge off, I'm gonna get something to eat. Take it easy, mother hen."

"No, you take it easy. I don't want you going back to work and getting yourself fired before you pay me back the money you owe me."

"Don't worry about me, I'll be just fine ... Hey look at that waitress, why couldn't she be our server, she's nice. Never had a waitress before, have you?"

"No Todd, I've never been with a waitress."

"Hey, maybe we can ask if she could be our server."

"Just calm down. We're here to eat not to pick up a date for you."

The waiter came back to their table. "One Sprite and water for you and double vodka on the rocks for you. Are we ready to order, gentleman?"

"Yes we are, I'm starving. I'll have the moo goo gai pan with wonton soup, thank you." said Jonathan.

"I'm gonna have the sushi roll, a cheese burger, and the shrimp salad." The waiter took the orders and walked off.

"So what do you think John? It's almost two o'clock. She still hasn't called. I think you'll be in the clear for tonight."

"Yeah, it's starting to look that way. She normally calls by now to confirm if were gonna hang out. She hasn't even called to say hello. I just don't know yet, still gonna wait it out though."

"Well, I'm hoping she doesn't call, I want us to go to this party, and I know, deep inside, you wanna go too, so I got my fingers crossed." Todd said.

"Yeah, I bet you do. All right, I'll admit, I do wanna go, but it's purely out of curiosity. I just gotta see how such a relatively young guy reached that high up in the corporate world and how he's living, I'm already a fan."

"Now you're talking, Johnny boy."

"We'll see what happens later, that's all."

"So what do you think of old man Simmons getting fired for watching kiddie porn in his office, what an idiot."

"Yeah, it's sad."

"Sad, hell I want his office, freaking perv, serves him right. What, are you feeling sorry for him too now, Jonathan?"

"No, I just think it's sad that he's got that problem, where he likes looking at little kids to get off."

"Yeah, well I think he's an asshole, so good riddance. Oh good, here comes our food."

"So it doesn't bother you that the guys sixty years old and probably going to jail for the next couple of years?"

"What is with you man, how can you feel bad for this guy, he's in his office looking at creepy shit on the Internet and I'm supposed to feel bad because he threw his life away at sixty? First of all, that was very stupid, I mean if you're going to do that, you certainly don't do it at work, on your work computer. Secondly, he's got a good profession, making a good living, and he's pretty close to retiring, and that's all he should've been thinking about. No, I'm not sorry. I just don't have any sympathy for that kind of crap, and I'm a little surprised at you for pitying him."

"Look, I don't pity him. I just find it sad and I hope he gets help for his problem. I just don't think jail is gonna solve the problem, that's how I feel."

"Oh yeah, well what kind of punishment would help, Jonathan? What do you want him to do, go sit on some psychiatrist couch and cry about how he's got a disease and how he can't help it? No, I don't think so. Man, I don't know about you sometimes. You seem to be getting weirder and weirder every day."

"Alright, let's change the subject, Todd."

"That's fine by me." They sat silently for a few seconds.

"Hey Did I tell you Emily brought up the getting-married thing again."

"No."

"Yeah she was saying how we been together a long time, and how she's ready to be married, were getting older, she wants to have kids, start a family, you know the same old song."

"Well, what did you say to that?"

"I just kind of blew her off, you know, I told her I didn't feel like talking about it right now?"

"Well, I think that's kind of fucked up don't you think she has a legitimate right to want something more. You know what's gonna happen, don't you, your gonna lose her."

"Nah, she isn't going anywhere besides, I'm gonna marry her, just not right now. I wanna save a little more, do everything right for her."

Jonathan looked at Todd with a disbelieving look. "Yeah, well, I think you just still wanna play the field, is what I think."

"Oh it's that too, but it's mostly the money."

Jonathan disagreeably shook his head as Todd laughed.

"Hey, if your gonna do it, you gotta do it right, you gotta prepare, and, the way she's talking, I'll have to get three jobs to pay for that wedding."

"What about her parents, couldn't they help out; she is their daughter, that's normally how it works right?"

"No, I don't think so. They're retired, living in Florida on a fixed income, they don't have any money. But it'll work out, we got plenty of time before we get hitched, besides if I really need money I know just where to get it, two places, one, I'll tap my 401, and of course there's always the B.O.J.K."

"The B.O.J.K. What the hell is that?"

"That's you, the bank of Jonathan Krause." Todd laughed.

"Get the hell outta here, now I'm paying for your wedding? No way."

"Hey, we better get back Jonathan, It's after two, and I have a couple of more accounts to settle before close today."

"Yeah I have a few clients I need to contact. Also, I got a newlywed couple looking start a portfolio, I wanna catch them today. Their leaving the country for a couple of weeks, so I wanna set them up before they go, you know how that can be."

"Yeah, so let's head back, tie up the loose ends, and then its home for a shit, shower, and shave, then party time Friday night in the Hamptons, yes baby!"

"Right." Jonathan said.

"Hey, don't sound so doubtful you're going, because it's starting to look more and more like you'll be hanging with me tonight after all. Stephanie hasn't called, and, if experience serves me correctly, she won't."

Jonathan looked over at the waiter and motioned for him to come to their table.

"Yes sir?" The waiter asked.

"We're done here, we just need the check."

"Right away sir."

"You're picking up the check, right John?"

"I guess I am, since you're broke."

"Ha, you're just too funny; you should do comedy with that outrageous sense of humor of yours."

The waiter came back to the table with the bill, Jonathan paid.

"What are you leaving the guy, a forty-dollar tip?"

"Yes I am."

"What the heck for?"

"It's what we always leave."

"No, we don't."

"Uh, yes we do. Normally we split the bill and the tip, but again, since you're a little short in the pockets."

"I'll be fine by next week. This is just a little financial setback for the moment."

The men walked out of the restaurant and walked back to the office. Azraa'el followed closely behind, listening to their conversation.

"So how are you getting into this party? I mean it's not like the guy invited you to his house or anything. You don't even know him, what are you just gonna show up there?" Jonathan asked.

"The way we're getting into the party is just go there tell the doorman or butler or whoever it is that's letting people in, what department and what floor we're from you know, and we're in. That's how he does it, only people who work with us would know about the party so it'll be cool, no suit and tie, casual all the way."

"So who else is going from accounting?"

"Oh man, all the guys, Brian Kilpatrick, Kevin Bostick, Steven Harris, and Willie Johnson, a.k.a. Willie bags."

"How'd these guys all get invited to the party? Man, I'm feeling out of the loop."

"The only one that got invited was Brian, he's in tight with the boss because he knows where to get good shit, and he brought some honeys to the last party and the boss really liked that. Brian told me and the rest of the guys how to get into the party, apparently the boss thinks the more the merrier, so it's OK for us to go."

"Sounds like it's gonna be a wild night." Jonathan said as they entered their office building."

"Brian said the parties are kick ass, he's been to about four of them already and now we get to experience it too my friend."

They boarded the elevator and took it up to their office. Jonathan had a concerned look on his face wondering about his girlfriend, wondering why she had not contacted him yet. They arrived on the floor, got off the elevator, and walked to their office.

"Hey John, it's two o'clock, I'll talk to you in a little bit. I wanna finish up this work and possibly leave by four this afternoon. You know the traffic will be crazy tonight you need to pick up the pace too."

"Yeah, that's a good idea." Jonathan sat at his desk working, checking the time, making phone calls intermittingly. He took breaks and sat thinking about why his girlfriend hadn't called him yet. The frustration started building as the time went by.

"She better call," he thought to himself. "Am I going to this party tonight? She better freaking call."

He looked at the clock on the wall it was three o'clock. He checked his watch as if it would tell him a different time he looked over at Todd. Todd smiled and pointed to his own watch, indicating that the workday was almost over. Jonathan nodded his head and gave a half smile. He continued staring at Todd. He chewed on the cap of a pen, as his thoughts went into overdrive.

"Something tells me going to this party is gonna be a big mistake, but I already told him I was going with him. How can I get out of this?" He sat back in his chair he looked at the picture of Stephanie pinned to the wall of his cubicle.

"I'll tell him I'm not feeling well, my food went down wrong ... Nah he won't buy that, I still got some more accounts to finish up." He sat still for a minute, thinking, his eyes, squinting, he rubbed his face into his hands, he rubbed his eyes until they turned red. He looked in his desk and pulled out a mirror, he looked into it and then ran his hands through his hair. He rose from his chair and walked slowly toward Todd's desk, his hand resting on his stomach, Todd looked at Jonathan walking toward him and looked away and then quickly looked at him again with a confused look.

"What the hell, hey you look like shit. What's the matter with you man?" Todd asked.

"I don't know, all of sudden I'm feeling like crap. I think it was the food." Todd looked at his watch then looked at Jonathan suspiciously.

"It's my stomach man, I feel like I have to throw up, you know?"

"Hey I got just what you need." He pulled open the drawer to his desk.

"I got some Mylanta and some antacid, which one do you want, they'll both work so take your pick, you know what, take them both, take a swig of the Mylanta and take one of the pills that should help."

Jonathan looked at Todd then looked at the bottle of pills. He poured two from the bottle and juggled them in his hand.

"You know I may not be able to go tonight if I can't get over this feeling," he said while rubbing his stomach.

"Oh there it is, you don't wanna go now, you come over here with that sick dog look because you're trying to back out of the party. Well you know what Jonathan, go home get under your blanket, get yourself some hot tea and soup and call your mommy Stephanie."

Jonathan stared down at the floor not wanting to look his friend in the eye, knowing he was aware of his trickery.

"Go ahead, tell her you were a good boy, you stayed home tonight when you could've gone to a party that could have helped your career, not to mention the beautiful women that'll be there, aw forget it man I'll go by myself." Todd slammed himself back down in his chair and went back to work; shaking his head in disgust, he ignored Jonathan standing there.

Now Jonathan feeling bad about his attempted deception tried to justify it.

"It's just, I still have a lot work to do man. Look, I'm sorry I lied to you, but really, I'm never going to close the deal on these new clients if I don't make contact with them today."

Todd waved his hand at Jonathan not wanting to hear his excuses. Jonathan turned and slowly walked away. He went a few feet and then stopped, turned, and approached Todd again.

"You know you talk about how this party is supposed to help our careers, when in all reality, were doing pretty good here. I don't know what help your talking about. I feel good about where I'm at with this company, so don't make out like we need to be at this party, like our jobs are on the line or something."

Todd stared at Jonathan for a few seconds then asked, "Are you done, I'd like to finish up because I'm out of here in about forty-five minutes with or without you."

"Well I guess you're going without me then."

"Well fine then!" Todd again went back to work.

Jonathan walked away shaking his head not understanding why it was so important to Todd that they should make it to the party, but his mind was made up that he wouldn't be attending.

Jonathan now back at his desk started shuffling through papers trying to find contact numbers.

He glanced at the picture of Stephanie, then looked at the clock on the wall and felt his anger towards her increase he thought to himself.

"You know what, if she doesn't call I'm not calling her either, fuck it." He sat down at his desk and went back to work.

An hour had passed and Jonathan noticed Todd walking over to him.

"Hey, I'm headed home. What are you gonna do, are you gonna go or what?"

"I can't man. I caught up with that couple and I pretty much have them set up, but I still have some more loose ends to tie up. I'll probably be here until six."

"Six, no way. Hey, has she called?"

"No."

"See, I told you man, she's not gonna call. You need to just come with us tonight and deal with her tomorrow."

Jonathan thought about it for a few seconds.

"Nah, I better not. I'm going to just finish up and go home. I'm really not in the mood to go out."

"Ok listen, I have the address to the place, I'm writing it down. Put it in your pocket, go home take a shower, and I'll bet you'll feel a lot better and you'll be ready to hang then."

"Whatever," Jonathan replied.

"So, I'm gonna catch a ride with Brian at about ten o'clock, but I'll call you before we go, just to make sure. Maybe you'll change your mind by then, OK?"

"Ok, but I doubt it."

"Don't say that just go home perk up and find something to wear. I'll see you later," Todd said as he walked backward toward the doors. Jonathan waved him off as if to hurry him along and went back to work. But, he didn't work very long, as soon as he knew Todd was away from the building he packed up his brief case and quickly left for home.

CHAPTER 4
THE PARTY

Jonathan took a car service from work to his home. He got out of the car and walked into the building. He pulled his keys from his pants pocket and opened his mailbox. He grabbed his mail and looked through it as he slowly walked up three flights of stairs that led to the top floor of his apartment building. He put the key in the door opened it and did what he always does, hit the light switch before entering, then stood in the doorway and did a quick view of the excessively large living quarters. He walked in, still scanning with his eyes; he removed his coat and hung it on a post, then walked around the place making sure things were as he left them before leaving for work this morning. He checked his answering machine for messages, there were none; he pulled his cell phone from his pocket, looked at it then placed it on the coffee table along with the few pieces of mail.

He walked into the kitchen, took a drinking glass from the cabinet, put three cubes of ice in it, grabbed a bottle of wine and filled the glass to the top. He drank the wine in one swallow, then poured another and walked back to the living room. He sat down on the sofa, kicked off his shoes, loosened his tie, and sipped the wine. Exhausted, he leaned his head back, closed his eyes and enjoyed the calm and silence of being at home.

A few minutes went by as he sat at the edge of the sofa tapping his fingers against the glass. He stood up and walked over to the stereo, turned it on, and programmed his music. He turned the volume up high; the music blared throughout the apartment. As he listened to the music, his mind began to wonder. "Come on Steph, are you gonna call or not?" he said aloud. He walked around the apartment, pacing anxiously.

Two hours passed. He stood in front of the large windowpanes in the living room. He pressed his hands up against the glass and looked out over the city as the day began to fade, he checked the time on his watch it was seven thirty. He thought on Todd's 'words, "She's not gonna call, just go with us to the party." He wanted to go, but he also wanted to be sure his girlfriend wouldn't call to meet him.

He walked away from the window, put his hand in his pocket, and pulled out the paper with the address to the party. "Fuck this," he said, and then walked to the bathroom and showered.

He came out of the bathroom with a towel wrapped around the lower half of his body. He walked to his bedroom and went through his closet; he grabbed a pair of jeans and a shirt and coordinated them on the bed. He nodded his head in approval and went back to the closet, grabbed a pair of shoes and lined them up alongside the pants and shirt. He stood in front of a full-length mirror on the wall, brushed his hair, splashed on some cologne, and quickly got dressed.

After dressing himself, Jonathan went back to the living room, sat down on the edge of the couch nervously, bouncing his leg up and down.

He thought aloud, "What am I doing, its nine o'clock, it's getting late; she hasn't called, so fuck it, I'm going."

He picked his keys and cell phone up off the table and put them in his pocket; he put on a jacket and walked toward the door. Before leaving, he turned and looked around the apartment. He put his hand behind his back, grabbed the doorknob, and turned it. He looked back at the telephone sitting on the table, he stared at it for ten seconds, wanting it to ring, yet not wanting it to ring—it didn't ring, he opens the door and walked out.

Jonathan arrived at the party by taxi, pulling up to a huge, well-lit mansion. The drive way was five-hundred feet from the curb to the house, columns to the left and to the right of the entrance to the yard, with statues of lions sitting atop each one. He walked to the gate and pressed the buzzer. A man watching surveillance from inside the house of all who arrived answered.

"Your name sir? The man asked. "I'm Jonathan Krause, from the accounting department. My office is on the twenty-fifth floor." The buzzer sounded and the ten-by-100-foot gate rolled back. Jonathan walked up the cobblestone driveway.

Lights set along the drive way guided his way and gave a dim view of the grounds, lined with flowers, manicured lawns, and ten-foot-high shrubs. Even in the dark of night, he found the outer appearance remarkable. He walked up to the door and rang the doorbell.

He could hear the melodic bells from outside the house. A servant opened the door. When Jonathan entered, he was quickly led to the left wing of the house. As he walked, he looked around, silently admiring the white marble floors, a spiral staircase, a crystal chandelier, a two-foot sculpture of the owner's head sat on an oak wood desk near the front door.

Jonathan was led through a set of doors and down a long, dimly lit corridor, and, as he walked the corridor, he could hear music. He walked down a flight of stairs and then to another long corridor.

He walked toward another set of doors; the music got louder. The servant opened the doors to a huge room, where seventy-five people were enjoying themselves, laughing, dancing, and toasting with drinks. The room was slightly illuminated with red and black lights. Sofas sat up against the walls. Men and women servants, barely dressed, were delivering intoxicants, liquids and non-liquids, to the patrons. The smoke-filled air was thick; this large room similar to a hall concealed ten other smaller rooms where one could take part in any number of indulgences. Jonathan peeked into each of these rooms and the look on his face showed he approved of this environment. He walked around the grand room looking for his friend Todd, after a few minutes, he found him.

"Well, look who showed up. I thought you weren't coming?"

"I got done what I needed to get done, so here I am," replied Jonathan.

"Yeah, but you told me you had a pile of work."

"Yeah Todd, I know, but there's always Monday my friend ...man there's a lot of women here, did you check out the side rooms? Some freaky stuff happening there."

"Hell yeah, and were gonna be a part of it," Todd said.

"No were not." Jonathan replied.

"We'll see about that."

"I'm telling you it's a little freaky for my taste." A woman approached the two men.

"Hello Todd."

"Hello Veronica," he replied.

"Whoa! She's hot man," Jonathan said.

"Yep...but not as hot as that one in the black dress and black pumps. Come on, let's get a drink." At that moment, the angel appeared.

Todd and Jonathan mingled with the crowd.

Azraa'el appeared sitting in a chair in the corner of the room but unseen, glancing at the partygoers. He focused his attention on Jonathan and spoke telepathically, calling out to him, "Jonathan."

Jonathan heard the voice over the music and commotion of the party; he looked around bewildered for a second, and then continued to mingle around the room.

Azraa'el called out again in the same manner as the first, "Jonathan." Again, Jonathan looked around to see who was calling his name; he walked over to the deejay and asked him why he was calling his name over the music. The deejay denied calling his name. He asked him again for reassurance, again he denied calling his name. He looked around the room; people were dancing and interacting with one another, and no one appeared to be trying to get his attention. He stood still and listened, but only heard music. He listened more intently and shook his head trying to get rid of the voice he knows he heard.

Todd walked over to him. "Hey man I got goodies." He waved a small clear bag in Jonathan's face. Todd had a woman on each arm, they made their way to a secluded area to ingest the contents of his bag. Jonathan indulged, after being persuaded by the woman. The spacious room, packed with people, started to look like a small dance club, men and women pressed up against each other, a hedonistic vibe pervaded throughout.

Jonathan and a young woman drew attention to themselves, groping and kissing each other while they danced, the effects of the intoxicants were starting to be felt.

Azraa'el walked through the Smokey room; he came up behind Jonathan and whispered, "Jonathan."

Jonathan turned around quickly, the clock showed twelve; Azraa'el waved his hand across the room and slowed the party atmosphere. The lights flickered, the music dragged, and the movements of all in the room slowed down. Jonathan was annoyed and confused.

"Have you been fucking with me all night, it's you, calling my name, isn't it?"

Azraa'el spoke and revealed the dreadful news, "Jonathan Krause I'm here to tell you what no man wants to hear, that you have ten days left on earth, ten days left to live, ten days of life."

"Who are you, what are you talking about, what's happening here, why is everyone moving so slowly?" He said as he looked around the room.

"Ah, you will get to know me very well soon enough, all questions will be answered, and all doubt removed, and, in ten days, life will end for you."

"You're a jerk; get the fuck away from me." Azraa'el began to give background on his subject,

"Jonathan Krause, NY, NY, 154 LISK ST. Apartment 3C, employed at Finch brokerage firm for six years, annual salary $170,000. No wife, no children, your mother and father are Alice and James. You have a younger sister, Jennifer, a girlfriend named Stephanie, and by the way, she's pretty fed up with you, in case you haven't noticed by now."

"OK, OK, what, ya wanna write my freaking life story, now what the hell do you want, this is weird," he said as he looked around the room.

"Your story has been written already, and we're approaching the last chapter my son."

Jonathan looked the angel up and down and circled him.

"What the hell are you talking about?"

"Why are you dressed like a priest, why did the room slow down, and why are you bothering me?"

Azraa'el made his introduction, "I'm a servant of the Most High, here to tell you, you have no more breath here on earth, you have no more food, no more drink anywhere throughout the universe, and your predetermined time is up. Your body will fail you and in ten days. I, Azraa'el, will return your soul back to its rightful owner, the Creator and ruler of all things." Jonathan didn't say a word. He stared at the angel with a serious look, and then exploded in laughter,

"So, what you're telling me is your nuts, your crazy right? Your one of those religious freaks, hey man you need a drink." The angel lowered his head, crossed his arms over his chest, and prayed, "Oh Merciful One, I seek protection from the one who tries to tempt your servant and lead him astray."

"You're hilarious, would you cut the bullshit already for Christ sake."

"Why do you call on the messiah in your state of intoxication, in this place of decadence, do you know him? I think not. He could not be of help to you in any way; no one can intervene for you."

"Alright, what do you want from me? I'm not here to talk about religion. It's a party man, and you're just ruining the fun. I was here with a cute girl, by the way where'd she go? We were having a good time, and then you showed up. I gotta tell you though, this is a neat trick you got going here, with the slow-motion action; it's weird but definitely cool…. Oh, I got it; Todd set this up, didn't he? OK, the jokes over, here's a few dollars, now go away and go have some fun."

The angel looked at the money Jonathan put in his hand with disgust and let it fall to the floor. "Indeed Jonathan, it is over, I've searched the entire universe to see if there was life for you anywhere, I found no life for you, your time is up, and you have ten days left in this realm."

Again, Jonathan laughed with disbelief.

"And after your ten days, I, lord of souls, will return you back to the Most High." The angel grabbed Jonathan's right arm and his right hand and said, "And now you will see things men should not see."

Jonathan's eyes widen, his hair stood up on his head. A small electrical current went through his body and he looked fearful and surprised simultaneously.

"Now enjoy your night," Azraa'el said as he let go of his hand and walked toward the door. "For every day afterwards, I will visit with you and review the work you have done while here in this realm. We have kept a record of you, and we are great at keeping the records of men—so prepare yourself my son, in a short time you will have no choice." Azraa'el waved his arm and the party resumed as it was. Jonathan looked surprised. The angel motioned his hand over his own face and body and he disappeared.

Jonathan stood there staring at the spot the angel had disappeared from; he questioned himself and wondered if the alcohol and drugs caused him to hallucinate this strange person. He moved slowly through the party and found his friends, who by now were also somewhat disoriented from the intoxicants.

"What's up, Jonathan? I'm in the back with these two 'chicks. They're ready to hang—let's go."

"Hey, did you see what happened here?" Jonathan asked as he looked around as if he were looking for something?

"No, what happened?"

"This guy was here. He was dressed in a white outfit, costume, robe thing, like the freaking pope, and ...and he told me I had ten days and ...and ...the whole party stopped moving, and he says he came to take my soul and I'm going to die in ten days. I'm telling you, this guy was weird. He walked over to that door and just disappeared."

"What guy, who you talking about Jonathan? I leave you alone for five minutes and you start seeing things. I think that hit you did is getting to you man, drink this—you gotta calm the fuck down, cause your killing my high dude." Todd said, as he handed him more drinks.

"No, I'm not seeing things. It was real man, and the guy went through that wall. What kind of shit did you give me, did you set this up Todd?"

"Set what up Jonathan, what the hell are you talking about man?"

"That could not have just happen—so you're telling me you didn't see everyone just kind of slow down, like slow motion, you didn't see that, don't you feel weird? ... I don't know man, maybe you're right. It must be the stuff."

"Yeah, I feel weird because I'm high as hell right now and you're killing it for me. You gotta relax dude. Let's go see the girls. They're waiting for us in the side rooms." Jonathan and Todd spent the remainder of the night with the women, and left the party at four a.m.

The next day Jonathan's girlfriend showed up at his apartment angry. She yelled to him from the street, and then pressed the buzzer to his door several times, but he didn't answer. She waited until someone exited the apartment building and walked in; she ran up the stairs and used the spare key she had to open the door. She entered the apartment and shouted for him as she walked around the place.

" Where are you? I know you're in here," she walked into the bedroom and yanked the covers off of Jonathan. He shot up and sat still.

"AHHH! Oh, hey honey."

"Who's in here in with you? I waited for you last night, but you didn't call, and your phone was off, so I came by here, what's going on? What were you doing that you were too busy to call me?" She asked angrily.

He paused for a moment breathing hard and sweating. "I was just having a terrible dream, we were going away on vacation together, we were going to Italy, but on our way to the airport, we got into an argument. So, I said I wasn't going and I left you at the airport because you told me you were still going on the trip anyway. So, I thought you got on the plane, and the plane we were supposed to be on crashed, doesn't even leave the tri-state area; 220 people died, no survivors! Man, it just seemed so real. I'm glad it was just a dream, I thought I lost you, but you're here and that's all that matters." She rolled her eyes at his story. As he hugged her, she didn't hug him back.

"Where were you, Jonathan?"

He thought if he should tell her the truth about what he was doing last night; his hesitation irritated her even more.

"Well, do you have anything to say?" She asked.

"Uh, well, for one thing, my phone definitely wasn't off, because I waited for your call all day yesterday, but anyway, uh, I was with Todd last night."

"What do you mean you were with Todd?"

"There was a party at one of our bosses' place."

"Oh, that's just great, Jonathan. Your friends are more important than me? That's typical of you, nice going!"

"No, sweetheart, it was a business party ... Oww, I'm hung over; my head is killing me." She punched his arm,

"It serves you right."

"Honey could you put some coffee on, and please, don't be angry, it was a business party. Look, some really weird stuff went on there."

"Yeah, I just bet it did," she said as she walked toward the door.

"I hope you had fun, when you're ready to be serious and stop acting like a teenager, give me a call ...good-bye." Jonathan got out of the bed naked and followed her to the door trying to convince her to stay.

"Honey wait, don't leave, let me explain, let me put some clothes on." He quickly walked back to the bedroom and put on the slacks he wore the night before, but while he went to the bedroom to get dressed, Stephanie left the apartment. He came back to the living room and noticed she had gone. He ran to the window and stuck his head out, and watched as she drove away.

" Honey WAIT! WAIT.... I'll CALL YOU!" He backed out of the window holding his hand to his head. The pounding headache was torture. He stumbled down the hall to the bathroom. He looked in the mirror, disgusted by his bloodshot eyes and messy hair; he let out a moan, "uhhhg." He threw water over his face, walked to the kitchen and grabbed the coffee pot; he filled it with water and sat it in the coffee maker, and then he checked his answering machine.

Message 1: "Hey, John, it's Bill. I hope you're almost done with those reports. We're really going to need them sooner than we thought, talk to you soon, take care buddy." 5:30 PM

Message 2: "Hello honey, where are you?"

Message 3: "John, it's me again we're supposed to see each other, did you forget?"

Message 4: "OK, this is my last call. Screw you," she said.

Jonathan stared at the machine with disbelief. He thought about how he waited for her call before leaving the house but no call. He looked at his cell phone and saw no missed calls. "Now how the hell did this happen?" He walked back to his bedroom and crawled into bed.

CHAPTER 5
ALL AT ONCE

Azraa'el stood atop a building with a legion of beings, one hundred to be exact. They focused their attention on a large aircraft. They watched as it cruised across the sky, cutting through the clouds. He spoke in a low tone and told the 220 passengers aboard, "Your time is up."

Azraa'el and the legion were unphased as they watch the plane make its fatal descent; all aboard will give their souls to the angel that day. Azraa'el and the legion spent time praying for each person. Then they moved hastily toward the terrible site to retrieve the dearly departed. When they arrived, emergency vehicles, and media surrounded the area.

Later that afternoon as Jonathan showered, flashes of the night before went through his mind. He was confused about the details of what took place. As the water splashed against his body, he couldn't help but wonder if what he'd seen was real or a hallucination. After a few minutes, he got out of the shower, wrapped himself in a towel and walked to the kitchen to get a cup of coffee, as he sipped, he walked to the front door and picked up his newspaper that lay just outside. He sat down on the couch and thumbed through it still, his mind could only focus on one thing, the angel. He thought for a few seconds then picked up the phone and called Todd.

"Hello."

"Hey, Todd. What's up?"

"What's going on, buddy, how are you feeling, great party huh?"

"Yeah, but what did we take man, I just feel a little strange still, you know."

"We had a little x, a little weed, and I guess a combination of the two might've fucked with you a bit because you went on a little trip."

"It couldn't have been just weed that was in it, it was just too crazy, and some guy shows up and ...."

"I know, I know, you told me. I think your imagination just got the best of you last night, that's all. 'How 'bout the 'chicks, I know you gotta remember that?"

"You know what, most of last night is a complete blur to me right now ...fuck!"

"Yeah, but you were a stallion dude. The girls really liked you, they want to hook up next week ,we gotta make that happen."

"I don't know man, Steph is pretty pissed at me right now, she says I blew her off yesterday and she came here and freaked out on me earlier. And that's the other thing, I know I waited here for her to call me before I left, and she didn't call. But, she says she called the house phone and my cell, I checked them both and I got no missed calls on my cell, but a bunch of messages on my home phone. Apparently, she called while I was still here, but I never heard the phone ring."

"Shit man, I hope you didn't tell her you were with me?" Todd said.

"Uh, yeah?"

"Aw come on, why'd ya do that, now she's gonna blame me for your screw up."

"So, what do you care, you don't have to deal with her, don't worry about her. I'll fix everything, I told her it was a business party."

"Yeah whatever, so what do you think, lets meet at the bar later?"

"I don't know, I told you, I gotta fix things with Steph."

"OK, fix things with her and then call me so we can meet up."

"Yeah, OK. Jonathan sat back on the couch for a few minutes and thought some more about the party. He giggled about the things he had done with the women, then got up and walked into the bedroom. He looked through his wardrobe and pulled out a shirt and a pair of jeans, he put on deodorant and cologne, and quickly got dressed. He walked back to the kitchen, refreshed the cup of coffee, turned on the T.V., and saw coverage of the plane crash; he watched the coverage, his jaw dropped, his mouth opened his eyes widen, he dropped the cup of coffee on the hard wood floors shook his head in disbelief and spoke out loud, "Whoa! But that was a dream, oh my god, I dreamed the plane crash, same amount of people, same destination holy shit!" He watched the coverage for an hour. He picked up the phone and called Stephanie; he got her machine and left a message.

"Stephanie, honey, I'm sorry OK, but please call me back, look at the news, my dream wow!" He hung up and changed the channel on the television and saw that every channel was covering the crash. After thirty minutes, he finally stopped watching. He got up from his couch and paced the floors for a few minutes, then walked over to the window and looked out.

Jonathan wondered how he could have such a horrible dream and more importantly have it come true. "What am I psychic now this is crazy?" He walked back over to the couch and sat down, his mind was racing, his thoughts were erratic, he started thinking about the angel, what he looked like, how the party atmosphere was slowed down, and what Azraa'el had said to him. Again, he turned on the television, pressed the buttons on the remote going through the channels; he stopped on a commercial, advertising life insurance policies. A man in the commercial offered policy quotes.

Suddenly Jonathan saw Azraa'el in the background of the commercial. Jonathan sat up quickly, 'his eye squinting, then open wide and filled with horror. As the man in the commercial spoke, he saw Azraa'el in the background and heard him telling a young boy he has just hours to live. He moved closer to the television. "What the fuck!" He said with confusion, and then Azraa'el looked into the camera and with an expressionless face waved to Jonathan then disappeared. He paced and thought to himself.

"No, this is not real, what the fuck is going on, who is this guy? No, I didn't just see that shit, oh my God, Todd what did you give me last night! It's the drugs it's gotta be the fucking drugs."

CHAPTER 6
LITTLE JAMES

It was a beautiful Saturday afternoon in New Jersey, three o'clock p.m. Azraa'el arrived at a park. He looked around and watched two women jogging around a track, a group of young men playing basketball, little girl's jumping rope as their parents watched and conversed with each other from a park bench. He walked over to an eight-year-old boy who was being pushed on a swing by another child. Azraa'el stood by as the boy swung back and forth, then made his acquaintance.

"Hi, James."

"Hi ...I remember you," the boy said.

"Do you, son?"

"Yeah, you're Azraa'el."

Azraa'el smiled at the boy and asked, "How do you know me son?"

"I know you from the garden."

"The garden?"

"Yeah, the garden we used to play together in, the one God built ...up there," he pointed and looked to the sky.

"You do remember me James. I remember you also."

"Yeah, it was a lot better there, smelled nicer too, not like here, pew." The boy said as he waved his hand in front of his nose. Azraa'el smiled.

"We can go back there, would you like that James?"

The boy jumped from the swing and stood in front of the angel.

"Really?" he said with excitement. "I would love to go there again, it would be fun, but will Brain ...Thomas, Christine, Andrew, and Joshua ...will they all be there too?"

"Brian will come later, but a lot of your other friends are there waiting to see you. They miss you."

"So why can't they come here?"

Azraa'el kneeled in front of James and put his hand on his shoulder. "You know why James ...don't you remember?"

James thought for a minute. "Yes," he said sadly. "I wanted to come here, and they wanted to stay there. I'm not afraid Azraa'el, but what about Mommy and Daddy, can they go with us? I have cool parents you would like them especially Dad, he's really strong"

"I'm sure I would James, but don't worry about Mommy and Daddy, they're going to come later. We'll go first and you can get things ready for them."

"OK, so are we going now, because I have to be in bed by 8:30?"

Azraa'el, held little James' hand, stroked his face, and said. "Tonight son ...you have ten hours left."

"Tonight, I don't know about that. I can't go out after dark. I'll have to ask Mom."

At that moment, James's mother called for him. He broke loose of Azraa'el's hand and ran toward her; he stopped short, turned around, waved, and shouted, "Good-bye, Azraa'el ,maybe I'll see you later!"

Azraa'el, with a sympathetic smile, waved and whispered as the child ran off, "Good-bye, James."

CHAPTER 7
ASRAA`EL'S SECOND IN COMMAND

Rafiqiel, Azraa`el's chosen second in command, travels the earth retrieving the souls of all living entities; he has dark skin, no hair on his head, and he is six feet five inches tall. He wears brown boots, white pants, and a white dashiki with a brown shawl that he wrapped around his neck. When speaking, his voice is always soft and in a low monotone. Rafiqiel travels on missions to and from the upper realm and loves being a soul collector. He appeared in Africa, sent to meet a young and powerful lion; the lion relaxing under a tree, hiding from the sun's heat, was disturbed by the presence of the great being. Rafiqiel, being a student of Azraa'el, was taught the science of physical transformation, and when he appeared, he appeared as a rival lion, and as he moved slowly toward his subject, the   lion roared to let the intruder know he was trespassing. Rafiqiel let out an even louder thunderous roar that shook the ground, then transformed into his true appearance. He stood within arm's reach of the lion and addressed him by name.

"Wusu, [the lion that goes to war], I am Rafiqiel, a servant of the Most High, second in command to Azraa'el the soul collector. I have been sent here to inform you that your time is up. You have two days of life left, then you will die, and I will return your essence back to the Supreme Being."

The lion stood still as if taking in the message of the messenger, then roared, and his roar was understood by Rafiqiel.

46

"No Rafiqiel, I am a great warrior and none of the four-legged creatures of this land can defeat me. I am the great warrior lion, I am a king, I will not die."

"It is true, Wusu, you are a great warrior, and it is true you are a king, but you know as well as I, there is a greater king than you, and that king says to me, your time is up." Rafiqiel turned and walked away. The lion let off a secession of roars in protest. Rafiqiel turned to face the lion and told him again, "You have two days," and he disappeared.

CHAPTER 8
THE SECOND VISIT

It is 6:00 p.m., Jonathan is unnerved by the vision he saw on his television screen earlier. He' has been pacing back and forth for hours, drinking coffee and water, trying to flush his system of the drugs he believes were the cause of his encounter with or apparent hallucination of Azraa'el. He counseled himself, "Alright. I gotta relax. It's not real; none of that shit was real last night. The guy isn't real, that slow motion shit at the party wasn't real, I got a little high and that's all it is. OK, so get that shit out of your head, Jonathan, be cool." He sat at his computer attempting to look up the side effects of the combination of drugs he had taken. He heard a knock at the door but ignored it and continued working. There was a second knock. He got up to see who it was. It was Miss Argento, an elderly but lively woman who lives in an adjacent building to Jonathan's; he helps her with her grocery bags from time to time.

"Hello Jonathan," she said as she walked into his apartment. "I'm returning the Frank Sinatra disk, thank you; my company and I really enjoyed listening to it."

"No problem, Miss Argento."

"Frank Sinatra is our favorite; I didn't know you had such good taste in music."

"Well, Mom and Dad played a lot of Frank and the boys around the house when I was growing up, so I guess it kinda stuck with me."

"A cousin and I saw him perform back in 1960, he was fantastic, all the girls loved Frank Sinatra, and, since all the girls loved Frank, all the guys wanted to be him. I miss those days, ah to be twenty-five again," she said with a look of reminiscing.

"Uh, Miss Argento, I'm kinda busy here," he said nervously as he looked at his watch.

"Oh I'm sorry, I'll let you get back to doing what you were doing, I have a nice tray of ziti in the oven. I'll bring some over for you later, OK?"

"Don't put yourself through all that."

"It's no trouble. I'll have enough to last a week."

"OK, Miss Argento. I'm gonna get back to work now."

"OK," she said as she walked toward the door.

" So when are you going to marry that nice girl, you're not getting any younger you know."

"Were working on it, Miss Argento."

"Well don't forget to send me an invite. I'd love to come to the ceremony."

"You got it. I'll see ya later," he said as he led her out the door.

"Good-bye, Jonathan."

Jonathan sat back down at the computer, pulled out his cell phone, and called his girlfriend, but he got the answering machine again.

"Steph, it's me, I'm trying to talk to you, I know your upset, but we have to talk, OK? I love you. I'll try you again later." He thought for a minute then started typing on his computer again. There was another knock at the door.

"Awe ...what now? He walked to the door and opened it, but no one was there, he closed it and got back to work. There was another knock at the door, he angrily got up to answer it, again, there was no one there. He stuck his head out the door, looked left and looked right, and saw no one, so he shut the door, turned around, and stood still. He scanned the apartment then ran over to the window, he looked down to the street but still didn't see anyone. He turned around and to his surprise saw the angel sitting at his computer, Jonathan shrieked loudly.

"Hello Jonathan," Jonathan stared at Azraa'el.

"Hey, you're the guy from last night. What the hell are you doing here, better yet how did you get in here?"

"Well, don't you remember our conversation from last night?"

"Yeah I do, now why are you are here, did Todd send you over here?"

"I was not sent by Todd."

"Alright then leave or I call the cops. I asked how you got in here," Jonathan reached into his pocket for his phone and found it smashed to bits and pieces. Staring at his smashed phone he screamed "What the hell! Look I don't have time for this, so what do you want from me?"

"I need to talk to you." The angel got up from the desk and looked around the room, and while his back was turned, Jonathan tried to attack him. The angel disappeared and then reappeared on the other side of the room.

"Do you think attacking me is a particularly smart thing to do? You're wasting time son. I just want to talk to you I want to let you know that I know all about you, who you are, the kind of person you've been, what you've done in this life. Your family, friends, co-workers, these people don't really know the real you, no not one of them can say they truly know the real Jonathan Krause, but I can; we can, because we see, hear, and know everything. This is a facade; you, are a facade. To make a person see you as something you're not, that's something you human beings are great at doing. You want people to think you're this great, helpful accountable guy, but that's not entirely true, is it?"

Jonathan walked over to the phone on the table and picked it up; the angel waved his hand in the direction of Jonathan.

"OWW! GOD DAMNIT. THAT BURNED!"

"I want your undivided attention."

"OK, OK, but you're freaking me out dude. I mean you want me to believe you're an angel? Look at you, last night you were wearing a bathrobe like some freaking warlock, today you're wearing a three-piece suit, you just appear out of nowhere. How the hell did you get in here anyway?"

They both stared at each other silently for a moment, Jonathan then suddenly made a dash toward the door attempting to leave the apartment he tried opening it, pulling and twisting on the doorknob but he was unable to.

"I have all the time in your world, so let me know when you're ready to begin."

"Begin what?" he said frustrated.

"Begin reviewing your work here on earth."

"Reviewing my work, what the hell does that mean? I'm not going to talk to you, I don't know you, how do you even know where I live? I want you to get out of my apartment. Angel of God, bullshit, more like bullshit artist trying to scam me for my money. Sorry pal, seen that trick before, so it ain't gonna work here."

"I'm Azraa'el, one of the four most powerful beings created by the Most High, unlike you I can only speak truth, and I'm in need of nothing man has to offer. I am a spiritual being from the spiritual realm; your material wealth means nothing to me." Jonathan annoyingly closed eyes and shook his head trying to comprehend the angel's meaning.

"What the hell do you mean you're from the spiritual realm?"

"I've come for your soul Jonathan and in ten days, you are going to die; we went over this last night and I don't think I can be anymore clearer."

"I'm gonna die ...So you're gonna kill me, you're here to kill me, is that what this is all about?"

"Far be it for me to commit murder, I don't kill men, I merely return the soul back to its rightful owner, back to the Most High."

"Bullshit. I'm not going anywhere."

"Funny how when it's your time to go you don't want to go. We know about your past Jonathan."

"What are you talking about?"

"You've done some terrible things in your earlier years, and its best that you confess these things before leaving this realm, for the good of the soul."

"Look I don't know what the hell you're talking about and I want you to get out of my apartment."

"I'm trying to help you son. This can be very easy or extremely difficult. My leaving now isn't going to change the outcome of your destiny. You have many things to feel ashamed of, the time is at hand where you will no longer be of this world, and your soul will reveal the truth of how you carried yourself in this life. I ask you again to relieve yourself of these dreadful secrets—there's one, that stands out above all. Confess and your soul will feel at ease."

"No, I'll feel at ease when you leave me the fuck alone, I didn't ask to speak to a priest, I have nothing to say to you, I don't know you, and I have nothing to confess. Even if I did, it sure as hell wouldn't be to you. Now if you don't mind, please leave and don't come here again."

"O, Jonathan, Jonathan, what you don't understand is you have no choice as to what's going to happen, but to show you the seriousness of why I'm here, my question to you is, do you remember Jimmy Benton?"

Jonathan gasped, his eyes open wide, he turned pale, and stared at the angel, not ever believing this man to be an actual angel, he thought the being in human form was there to do him harm. He became worried and backed away from him, trying to put a barrier between them; he stood behind the desk looking very afraid.

"Well, you do know him, don't you Jonathan?"

"Uh, yeah, I knew him a long time ago, back when I lived in Kansas, is that why your here?"

"There was a movie out sometime ago, what was it called, oh yes, I Know What You Did Last Summer, or something like that, right? Well I know what you did every summer, particularly that summer, but I'm not here because of Jimmy. I'm here to return you to the

Most High. I'm mentioning Jimmy to let you know that we are aware of everything that goes on, not just this realm but every realm. Before I retrieve a soul or an essence, I am fully aware of the person; this way there can be no twisting of the truth. Oh, but many try to deceive anyway, and only deceive themselves, But so far, my son, you have made your mark in this world, to bad none of it was for good."

"Yeah, big deal you know who Jimmy is, what does he have to do with anything"?

"Well it's nice to see how casually you brush off how you treated one of your closest friends, but then again why would I expect you to have any compassion, that is not who you are, at least not yet."

Jonathan walked to the door, pulled hard, he kicked at it, the door opened; he motioned for the angel to leave.

"Hey, do you mind? I'm not in the mood. I really don't want to be bothered right now, just go already." But, the angel ignored his request and walked around the apartment looking at pictures, touching the table decorations, and taking in the scene of the place. "Do you remember the words Jimmy said as you and your buddy Michael Pratsky did what you did to him, dragged him kicking and screaming? "No stop, please don't," those were his words, am I correct? You two were a real piece of work and only twelve years old, you got started pretty early."

Jonathan was shocked by the angel's knowledge of the other childhood friend Michael; he stood silent, watching the angel roam his apartment, and then he closed the door.

"You two bullied that kid and never let up."

"Who told you that?" Jonathan asked.

"Well, your soul was distraught about the things you were doing to people and while you slept, it came to us and pleaded forgiveness about what it was made to be a part of, not to mention the fact we had to stand by and watch you do these things."

"Who told you that? That's not true, that's not true!"

"Ah, Jonathan, do you think I just pulled these acts out of the air? Besides, Michael Pratsky died in an automobile accident two year after you relocated to this part of the world, and when he came back to us, his soul beard witness against him. In the upper realm, no lie can live. The soul that lives inside you belongs to the Most High, Before it can reconnect to the Supreme Being, it bears witness to what it took part in, while it walked with its temporary owner—a cleansing of the soul, if you will. So, while you try to disassociate yourself with what you are charged with, know that your soul will abandon your lie and reveal the truth." Jonathan was frozen, yet shaking with fear.

"Be at peace Jonathan, I'm not here to hurt you. I told you, I'm here to talk."

"I'm sorry ...I'm sorry ...we were just kids, we didn't know it would turn out that way, we were just messing around you know, kids' stuff. We weren't trying to hurt anybody."

"Yes, typical answer that man gives, 'wasn't trying to hurt anybody, I didn't mean to hurt anybody,' yet someone is hurt, someone did get hurt."

"So, is this why you're here, because of that?"

"No. What's done is done."

"Then why ...why me, why'd you pick me to come after, I mean there are hundreds of thousands of people who are gonna die in ten days, millions maybe, why are you singling me out?"

"None of this happens suddenly, don't think you're some special case because you are not. I'll be visiting many like you over the next ten days, I do this every day, You're not special. I'm here because I felt a need to talk to you personally. How a young guy like you, in a very short time, managed to cause so much destruction and pain to other people, but you human beings, this is what you do, you cross every boundary without discretion.

I've seen all the conditions and burdens man puts upon himself, but nothing short of being told, you're going to die, will change the direction of the way you behave toward each other, and it grieves us to no end. To know how much the Most High cares and loves you, and yet many of you show very little gratitude, if any at all."

"Yeah GOD loves us, loves us so much. Look at all the crap that goes on in the world, and you're gonna tell me how God loves us?" Jonathan stood back in fear of the angel as he spoke his words.

"You doubt because everything can't be perfect in your world son."

"No. I doubt because of the bullshit that happens every day throughout this hell hole we live in, little kids being kidnapped, people being murdered, woman being raped, wars being started by every little ass-backward country, yeah God really cares, sure he does," he said with sarcasm.

"And you certainly contributed to some of those crimes didn't you Jonathan ...speaking of rape, would you care to tell me about the one you committed?"

"Now what are you talking about? I didn't rape anyone."

"I'm certain you did." Azraa'el pointed his finger at the television, it came on, and the screen showed Jonathan dropping a pill in a young woman's drink. Jonathan again is surprised by what he is being shown; shaking his head in shame, he stared at the short film of himself.

"You must confess this crime Jonathan and cleans your soul."

"Hey, we were hanging out and she wanted to have a little fun. I certainly didn't rape her."

"No son, you know like I know, she had no idea you poisoned her drink, and if you were just going to be hanging out, how come she's unconscious only a half hour after meeting up with you. Your lies will be revealed. That's the date rape drug, and you took advantage of her while she was out. Do you still blame God? The Most High didn't make you rape that girl, didn't make you do what you did to Jimmy either, that was you and Mikey."

"Hey we remained friends. I saw her couple of times after that."

"Yes, because she's not sure about what happen that night, but we know what happen that night, this crime makes you a rapist."

"I didn't rape her, I just helped her relax."

"Yes, you helped her relax, and then helped her into your bed."

"No, I don't see it that way."

"Of course you don't, but maybe if it was your mother or your sister, or that pretty little girl friend of yours, you might see things differently ...confess your sins son." Jonathan glared at the angel but knew he was right.

"Alright ...alright, I'm sorry!"

"Don't apologize to me, I'm not the one you violated. You people think saying sorry will fix everything."

"I know I haven't been perfect."

"To say the least."

"I'm just trying to come to grips with this whole thing. This is just so crazy. I can't handle this man. Could you leave? I would appreciate it if you left, I need to be by myself."

"Sure, Jonathan. I'll leave. Its time you come to grips with the real you; you're not the first to have to look in the mirror and see the real person."

"By the way, was that you I saw on the commercial? I thought it was my mind playing tricks on me. That wasn't you, right?" Azraa'el stared at Jonathan.

"It was not your mind playing tricks on you, Jonathan."

His jaw dropped, Sadness came over him, and he asked, "But how ... how did you do that?"

"Because I am who I say I am, that's how. I told you last night, now you will see."

"See what?"

"You will see what I see ... death." The angel grinned at Jonathan.

Jonathan shook his head in disagreement with the angel's decree. The pupils of his eyes darted side to side nervously.

"But I don't want to see death," he said with a childlike innocence. "Why would I want to see that? Hey, you had a little boy in that commercial. Are you going to kill that kid? Oh shit, you're going kill a little kid!"

"I don't take the lives of any living being, but, yes, the boy's soul will leave with me tonight.

He stared at the angel suspiciously, and then with a slight laugh said, "Nah this is all bull shit. I don't know why I'm getting all rattled by you, because you're not real. What kind of name is Azraa'el anyway? You're not a real person. Jonathan walked over to the door and once again motioned for the soul collector to exit his apartment.

"OK then, good-bye, Jonathan, but know with certainty you have ten days left."

"Yeah, whatever."

Azraa'el left the apartment, and Jonathan slammed the door shut.

CHAPTER 9

EARTH'S LOSS, HEAVEN'S GAIN

Little James Washington was the only child of Andre and Beverly Washington, his father a thirty-five-year-old mechanic shop owner and his mother a part-time schoolteacher. They lived in a modest house on the outskirts of Jersey City, New Jersey. They loved bike riding and going to the park on the weekends as a family. On that Saturday, James's dad had opened his auto shop at 7 a.m., as he does every weekend, so he was not around for the meeting little James had with Azraa'el. His father arrived home at 9:00 p.m. that evening. His wife greeted him.

"Hey big man."

"Hey baby."

"How was your day today?" she asked as she unbuttoned his shirt.

"Today was great, but coming home to you just put the icing on the cake," He hugged and kissed her.

"What's for dinner?"

"Hey, you have a son in there who was asking to see you earlier, says he wants to say good-bye to you."

"Good-bye?"

"Yeah, he thinks he's going out to see his friends later. That boy has too much energy and a wild imagination."

"Let me go see what's up with my boy. Hey babe, kinda hungry."

"I'm on it," she replied. James's dad walked into a dark bedroom, turned on the light, and walked over to his sleeping son, he wiped the sweat from the child's forehead and woke him with a kiss on the cheek.

"Hi, Daddy."

"Hey, little man."

"I tried to wait up for you, but I got sleepy."

"I know son, I got a little caught up at work."

"We missed you today. I wanted to play catch with you, but you were working so me and mommy went to the park. I saw one of my old friends I haven't seen in a long time. I'm supposed to meet him later to see my other friends."

"Oh yeah?"

"Yeah, but he better hurry up cause it's already past my bedtime," he said as he yawned.

"Maybe you can go see your friend's tomorrow, son."

"Yeah, I'm sleepy anyway, good night Daddy."

"Goodnight, son," he kissed his son on the forehead and walked back into the kitchen.

"Hey babe, he feels a little warm, little sweat beads rolling down the boy's forehead."

"Sit down and eat, I gave him some children's Tylenol. He'll be fine. He goes through that sometimes. I'll keep an eye on him."

"OK, you keep an eye on him, and I'll keep an eye on you." He said flirtatiously. Later that night, James's mom woke from her sleep to use the bathroom, but before going back to bed, she walked into his room, put on the light, and then walked over and felt his forehead. He felt very warm ,he called out his name. "James," he didn't respond. She shook him and screamed his name, "JAMES! She sat him up and pulled him close to her, wiping the sweat from his face, his dad ran into the room.

"What's the matter?"

"I can't wake him; he's burning up with fever!"

"Alright, get him dressed. We gotta get him to the hospital," his dad said. They put on their bathrobes and ran to the car and laid little James in the back seat. They drove frantically and arrived at the hospital in fifteen minutes. James's dad carried him in; his mom was crying as the nurse came over.

"What's the matter?" she asked.

"He's running a fever, he's burning up, he's not responding to me," the boy's mother replied.

"Are you the parents?" the nurse asked as she listened to his heart with her stethoscope.

"Yes," the mother replied.

"How old is he?"

"He's eight."

"When did you realize he was feverish?"

"He was a little warm earlier this evening but not this bad."

"Is he taking any medication right now?"

"Just children's Tylenol."

"Is he allergic to any medication?" she asked while motioning for someone to bring over a bed for little James.

"No."

"OK, let me have him dad, give the receptionist all of James's information including your insurance. Mother come with me were gonna go in and take care of him."

"Please help him, I don't want to lose my son!" his mother begged.

"OK, were gonna do everything we can do for him."

The nurse took James to an area with many beds, and laid him on one them. They took his blood pressure it was normal, everything about him was normal, except him feeling extremely warm so they put him in a tub of cold water that brought his fever down but ten minutes after bringing it down it would rise again. His battle for life would continue through the night, the nurses and his mother used cold towels, ice packs and giving him fluids through I.V. All the while Azraa'el paced back in forth in the room watching closely. They worked on James into the late morning hours, moving him to a room as his condition would not improve nor did it get worse. The doctor had gone home, nurses took long breaks, and his mother although sitting in the room with him, was exhausted emotionally and fell asleep. And now, no one aware or attentive, James's fever rose beyond saving, and the machine little James was hooked up to indicates he has now died. His mother jumped up looking terrified and screaming, nurses and doctors come rushing in, his dad runs toward his son's room but nurses and the other staff hold him back from entering the room. Now, they make his mother leave the room also. They pound on his chest giving him oxygen but the machine is still indicating Little James is gone. His mother outside the room pacing and not wanting to watch what was going on starts to pray but his dad looking through the window watched their son's fight for life end. He turned around and walked slowly toward his wife, his eyes staring down at the floor, the defeat and pain on his face alarmed his wife. She ran toward the I.C.U screaming hysterically James's dad grabbed her and hugged her tightly, with contained emotion and tears coming down his face, they both collapsed to the floor. His mom, heartbroken, screamed out for her only child.

"NO ...NO, James!"

Immediately his dad visualizes the times he had with his son: playing catch, teaching him how to ride his bike, wrestling in the yard, the family walking through the park. A blank stare on his face, the mother is inconsolable; as the doctor came toward them, his father already accepting his son was gone, she snatched her hand away from her husband and quickly rose to her feet with hope in her eyes.

"Doctor, please, tell me he's OK."

"We did everything we could, I'm sorry."

His mother became more hysterical. As Azraa'el held the soul of the excited jovial boy, the angel shielded his eyes and ears so he would not see or hear his heartbroken parents crying out for him.

CHAPTER 10

THIRD VISIT TO JOHNATHAN

J onathan had been feeling a bunch of emotions since his first meeting with the angel. Even after being shown many of the things in his past, he was still in doubt of Azraa'el's intentions. Nevertheless, a couple of days have gone by, and an uneasy feeling set upon him. He sat around his apartment wondering mostly, if this man claiming to be an angel was really an angel or just a crazy person trying to extort money from him. What intrigued him most is how this man knew of his past transgressions, being that he never spoke about them to anyone; his sinful acts always left him feeling a little ashamed when he did think about them. As he thought on the words of the soul collector, Azraa'el would enter his thoughts and remind him saying,

"Confess before you die, confess, confess." He banged his hand against his head to rid himself of this voice.

He wanted to talk to someone, anyone, so that his mind would stop focusing on the angel. He made a phone call to his friend Todd, but he didn't answer. He tried to reach his girlfriend by telephone, also, but she didn't answer either. Escaping the thoughts in his mind was impossible, and Azraa'el continued to send telepathic messages to him, "You have eight days left to live."

"Get the fuck out of my head, leave me alone!" he shouted as if speaking to someone in the apartment. Then 'he started wondering if this is all true. "How will I die, is this man going to try to kill me? Am I sick? Will I get hit by a car? No, this is all bullshit, it can't be real."

He grabbed the newspaper, sat down on the couch, and slowly looked through it; he came across a small headline, 8-Year-Old Dies of Pneumonia. He flips to the next page, then quickly went back to the article about the boy and read it.

"Was that the kid I saw on the television screen with this angel guy?" Jonathan's face filled with horror as he reads more of the article.

"No, the kid died in the hospital." He sat still for ten minutes picturing the boy and the angel in the commercial. He then went to his computer and looked up angels. Images of lesser beings appeared on the screen, along with the rebellious angels.

He thought on the soul collector's name and typed it in; an image appeared, and under the image was the title Angel of Death. They also gave a list of responsibilities associated with Azraa'el, and some descriptions unbefitting the lord of souls, such as death lord, dark angel, and grim reaper. Jonathan sat back quickly in his chair and stared at the screen.

He thought, "The words used by this man to describe himself match some of the description on the computer, yeah but he could have come here and looked this page up the same way I did. But damn, this is a little eerie. He knows too much about me, and there's no way for him to know these things. I never spoke about this stuff to anybody, not even Mom and Dad." He closed the computer and paced back and forth. "Eight days left," he thought.

"I better go make a police report on this guy, he's too creepy." Jonathan called the police department and asked how he could report someone threatening his life. They took him seriously until he told them the person claimed to be an angel, then he was ridiculed but he was still told he could come to the police station to make the report.

He sat quietly for five minutes after the embarrassing phone call, then had an idea to go see his doctor. He figured if he had some kind of undetected illness that would cause his untimely death, he'd better try and catch it before it was too late. He called his doctor's office.

The answering service told him that the doctor was working in the hospital that day. He left immediately for the hospital, a forty-minute ride on his bike. He arrived and walked straight to the receptionist.

"Hi, I need to see Dr. Basheer."

"Third floor sir, take the elevators."

Jonathan got on the elevator and took it to the third floor. He got off, walked over to the nurse's station, and asked for the doctor.

"Hello, nurse. I need to see Dr. Basheer."

"And who are you sir?"

"My name is Jonathan Krause. I am one of Dr. Basheer's patients."

"Are you a patient here at the hospital?"

"No."

"Well the doctor is seeing patients. You'll have to see him at his office."

"No, I have to see him today, and I have to see him right now."

"I'm sorry sir. He's visiting patients, and we don't disturb the physicians when they're making rounds."

"OK, I can page him ...he's a doctor, he has to answer his pager."

"If you want to page him sir, that's up to you, but we cannot page doctors for people who just come in off the street." He became annoyed, "He's my private physician and I need to see him!"

"You'll have to see him at his office sir. If you need his office number, I can get that for you."

"I have the number; I called the office. They said he was here and that I should come here, OK?"

"Well, they shouldn't have told you to come here, sir. That's not how it works."

"He's on this floor, right? Then I'll just wait for him ...I'll just wait."

Jonathan waited two hours before the doctor finally came to the nurse's station; he got up out of his chair and rushed over to him. "Dr. Basheer!"

"Hey, Jonathan, how are you buddy?"

"Doc, I really have to see you, I need your help. I could be deathly ill."

"Well, what's the problem, Did you hurt yourself, What's wrong?"

"I don't know doc, but I need you to check me out fully. It can't wait."

"Jonathan, what have you done?" The doctor asked with a smile. "OK, come to my office tomorrow."

"No, no, no, I need to know today," Jonathan grabbed the doctor by the arm.

"Please doc, can we do a full check-up today?"

The doctor paused before answering, "OK Jonathan. Nurse, put Mr. Krause in room 212. I'll be examining him."

"Thank you doc, thank you."

The nurse walked Jonathan into a room and told him to change his clothes; he took off his clothes and put on a hospital gown, irritated by the unwelcome news and recent turn of events, he couldn't keep his mind off the angel. He lay down on the hospital bed and stared at the ceiling, thinking, how he was going to get to the bottom of this today.

"Okay Jonathan, were going to do a blood test, urine analysis, check cholesterol, EKG all of that good stuff, OK?"

"OK doc, can we put a rush on the results?"

"Well, the tests are going to take a couple of days to come back. Is there something you want to tell me Jonathan, is there something I need to know, what's this panic all about?"

"I ...I've just been really stressed out over the past few days you know, I may have lost my girlfriend, I have some deadlines at work coming up, it's hard for me to sleep at night."

"I've actually been awake for the past two days. Sometimes, my breathing, it's ...it's hard to breath." He became short of breath, he bent over resting his hands on his knees trying to recover. The doctor was alarmed.

"Jonathan, you look a little more than stressed. Are you sure that's all you're feeling?"

"Well, no. I was at a party a few nights ago, I smoked some marijuana and since then I been feeling weird."

"Are you sure that's all you did? Maybe someone gave you something more powerful without your knowing what it was. Are you sure?"

"I'm sure doc, I was with some friends. We all smoked the same thing, and everyone else is fine. I've just been feeling weird and I'm a little worried," Jonathan kept the appearance of the angel from the doctor.

"OK, were going to run some test on you, but I'm sure you just need a little rest. Drugs affect people differently. You have to be careful with that stuff. OK, just try to relax now; the nurse will come in a little while to get you for your exam."

"OK doc, thanks for seeing me today."

"No problem, buddy."

Jonathan hoped the doctor was right about just needing some rest; he was checked and tested for two hours.

"OK, were all done. We can't tell right away what the test results are; it takes a couple of days. Don't worry. You're not going anywhere in two days, right?"

Jonathan thought about the angel telling him he has ten days, he counted to himself using his fingers.

"Uh, no doc, I should be here. I should be here right?"

"Take it easy Jonathan, I'll call you in a couple of days, OK?"

"Ok, good-bye doc, and thank you again."

"See my nurse before you leave. I wrote you a prescription for valium to help you relax."

"Thank you doc, thanks a lot."

Jonathan left the hospital and started heading home on his bike. On his way, he began to count the days since his last talk with the angel.

"That was two days ago. Damn, if I'm gonna die two days have gone by. The doc said he would call me in a couple of days; shit, that only gives me six days. I gotta call Stephanie."

He picked up speed, anxious to deal with this situation, still believing there's a solution to it all. Jonathan arrived home; he immediately grabbed the phone and called Stephanie.

"Hello ...Steph."

"What is it Jonathan?"

He smiled and put his hand over his heart.

"Oh honey, you don't know what I been going through here."

"Oh, I don't know what you been going through , You got a lot of nerve, Jonathan. You completely blow me off, don't return any of my calls so that you can go hang out with your friends at a fucking party, oh excuse me, business party—well you can just go to hell. I don't need your bullshit!"

"Steph, I'm dying."

"What?"

"I'm dying. I just came from the hospital and had a complete check-up and."

"Yeah, whatever Jonathan. This is just some more of your bull to get back into my good graces."

"No, no Steph, please, I really need to talk to you, I need you, please, I'm begging."

"Why Jonathan, why should I care? You didn't care."

"I know, but please, I'll do anything."

She thought for a few seconds before responding to him. "I don't know, what you did the other night, just tells me you don't care, you just don't care about us, well I should say me, because it was me who got stood up, and I'm still angry with you."

"I'll make it up, just come over, OK?"

"Look, I'm kinda busy today. I can't talk right now."

"Steph, I need you now."

"Oh, you need me now, why, so you can tell me about your phony doctor visit to suck me back into your little childish games, not this time, buddy."

"No, not at all, just please meet me tomorrow and I'll be able to explain in person, just promise you'll come by tomorrow, this is very important."

She paused, closed her eyes shaking her head no, feeling like she shouldn't be bothered with him, but she gave into his request. "OK, I'll come by tomorrow," she said in a threatening manner, but if this is some more of your bullshit, I swear to God, it'll be the last time you ever see me, and I mean it!"

"No Steph. This is no bullshit. I'm very serious. I have to see you; do you promise you'll come see me?"

"Yes, I promise I'll be there. Unlike you, I keep my word, now I gotta go, I'll talk to you later."

"OK. I love you Steph."

"Yeah, whatever," she slammed the phone down as Jonathan sat back on the couch.

He thought for a minute then called Todd.

" Hello."

" Hey man. It's me."

"Dude, I've been calling your house, your cell, a couple of days now. What's going on?" Todd asked.

"You gotta promise not to freak out on what I'm about to tell you Todd."

"Okaaay?" he said curiously

"No, promise me you'll hear me out?"

"You got my word. I'll listen and I won't freak out."

"Alright, remember that guy I was telling you about, the guy from the party?"

"Yeah."

"Well, he showed up at my apartment, and everything he said to me that night, he said again here. We started talking, and the guy knew things about me that no one knows. He did some stuff with the T.V."

"What are you talking about Jonathan?"

"He showed me on T.V., doing something with a girl, a couple of years back. It was like a movie. I stood there and watched myself from like five years ago doing something I probably shouldn't have done."

"You know what you sound like right now, Jonathan?"

"Yes. I know, but he came here, and that's what he showed me. If I didn't see it for myself I wouldn't believe it either. At the party, he grabbed my hand, my arm, and told me now I will see what men shouldn't see."

"Yeah, and what the hell does that mean?"

"At first, I didn't know, but now I know what he meant. He made me psychic."

Todd laughed. "Oh, brother would you stop it, you sound ridiculous, Jonathan."

"No, hear me out; did you see the plane crash coverage?"
"Yeah, I looked at it this morning for a few minutes, what about it?"

"I dreamed about that plane crash, the amount of people on the plane, how there were no survivors, I knew the airline, where it was departing, where it was arriving, the times everything. I fucking dreamed about it!"

"So, you had a dream, doesn't mean you're psychic. You could have heard the news in your sleep. Did you go to sleep with the T.V. on?"

"See that's the thing, I was dead asleep. Lights were out; shades were pulled, complete silence and darkness."

"That was just a coincidence, Jonathan."

"No way, I don't think so, I think he's serious He also said. ..." Jonathan held his words for a moment and thought of how to tell his friend.

"He also said what?" Todd asked.

Jonathan, with fear in his eyes, responded, "He also said I'm gonna die in a few days."

"See right there is when you should have put him out of your fucking house and called the cops on the crazy bastard."

"Oh, I called the cops right after he left here."

"What did they say?"

"They basically laughed at me, told me if I wanted, that I should go down and make a report, but I felt like I'd just be wasting my time."

"This is weird, and I don't believe any of it."

"Yeah, I know Todd; you've always been supportive that way," Jonathan said sarcastically.

"Come on man, you just said you wouldn't believe it if you hadn't seen for yourself, so what do you wanna do?"

"Come over, I'll finish telling you what he told me."

"Alright, I'm gonna get on the train. Be there in about a half hour."

After Jonathan got off the phone with Todd, he thought about revealing his past to his friends and family. What to say and when to do it was his dilemma. He thought for a while longer then dialed his parent's phone number, his mother answered.

"Hello Mom."

"Hello son, how are you?"

"I'm fine ...uh I'm gonna need to come over tomorrow."

"What do ya mean, tomorrow, you normally come on the weekend, don't you have to work?"

"Yeah, but I'm not going in. I'm really gonna need to talk with you and Dad."

"Jonathan, what's wrong?" she asked with concern.

"It's nothing, I just have to talk to you guys, OK? So let Dad know. Do me a favor, call Jen, she should be there for this too."

"Well, what's going on? You're making me nervous."

"Don't worry Mom, everything's fine. Just ...I'll be over tomorrow."

"OK. If you say so Jonathan. What time are you gonna be here?"

"I don't know yet, but I'll call before I come."

"OK son, I love you. I hope everything is fine, but it doesn't sound like it."

"Don't worry Mom, Love you too, Bye."

Jonathan called his job then remembered it was Sunday; there's no one in the office. He sat at the kitchen table spinning the top from a soda bottle, thinking to himself.

"What can I do to stop this craziness, how did this guy come into my life, what the fuck man, I have a great job, great girl, great place, why me? I guess this is my life, my punishment, shit I did in the past," There was a knock at the door.

"Who is it?"

"It's me man, open up.

Jonathan opened the door and let Todd in.

"So what's going on?"

"I don't know. I'm coming apart here."

"Well, what's up, what's the deal with this guy you say is coming for your ass."

"Hey, dude, it's not a fucking joke. This guy is serious, and I'm shitting my pants thinking about all the crap he told me. The guy ran down some really crazy things that happen in my past, like when I was a kid you know."

"Well, what was he saying?"

"Something's no one knows about me."

"Yeah, like what?"

Jonathan inhaled deeply and looked at Todd wondering how his friend would feel about the secrets he was so reluctant to speak about.

"No, I ... I can't talk about it right now, just some things I don't like talking about, that's all. You gotta see this guy man he's weird. I think he hates my guts. I think he enjoys fucking with me, ya know."

"Hey, do you really think you're gonna die? I mean, come on, some guy comes up to you and tells you he's an angel. Where have we seen that before. Hey, I'm Jesus Christ, I have the keys to life, I can tell your future. You know what I mean? Why are you believing this bullshit?" Todd said with a smile on his face.

"Because I know he's real, fucking guy showed up here and just appeared out of nowhere and how the hell did he know where I lived anyway, because I sure as hell didn't tell him."

"Yeah well, it still sounds a little wacky to me, like one of these phony-ass psychics looking to scam people. Don't get suckered."

"I know, I thought the same thing, but he hasn't asked me for anything, no money, no food, no clothes, nothing. He seemed very serious about what he was saying to me. Honestly, I'm afraid of him."

"You sure this guy's not some freaked out devil worshiper, maybe he worships Satan, looking for a new recruit?" Todd said jokingly.

"You know you can be a real smart ass at times Todd, but no. The first time I saw him, he talked about God, how we don't appreciate what God has done for us. This angel, man, whatever the heck he is, doesn't like human beings. I know it."

"And he's an angel huh? Sounds more and more like the devil to me. I think this is all pretty stupid, but hey I'm not the guy he's after," Todd continued with his sarcasm.

"Fuck you, Todd! I'm glad you find this amusing, but it's me he's messing with."

"Alright, alright, it's just so crazy you know."

"Yeah, I know that, but when the guy starts telling me about the worst time of my life, it makes me a little worried." Jonathan flopped down on the couch with a concerned look on his face.

Todd walked to the kitchen and opened the refrigerator.

"Where's the beer?"

"On the bottom rack."

"So what else did he say?" Todd asked as he opened two bottles of beer.

"He told me he would come here every day until I die. Can you believe that shit!"

"No, I can't."

"Well, I went to see my doctor, had him check me out, see if there was anything wrong with me, if I'm gonna die, maybe I'm sick, and I just don't know, I don't feel sick, I'm not in pain or anything."

"Don't talk like that, conjuring up your own death, cut that shit out, that's how Biggie and Tupac died, always rapping about their own death, don't do that man," Todd handed Jonathan a beer and sat down on the couch next to him.

"Well I took a bunch of test. I won't know anything for a couple of days. The doc thinks all I need is a little rest and relaxation from the drugs you gave me."

"So what, you're blaming me for this craziness now?"

"Yeah, well I was fine until I took all that shit you gave me."

"Hey, no one held a gun to your head, besides I had the same stuff, you don't see me acting schitzo."

"Yeah, I wonder why?"

"So that's how it is now, huh? I gave you some bad shit, I wouldn't do that to you man, and it's fucked up you even think that I would."

"I just want some answers, dude. Have I been that fucked up in my life that it has to come to this? I wouldn't even be so worried except for the thing he did with the T.V, the dream and him knowing all about me.

"It's not gonna happen, stop talking like that. I'm here to help anyway I can. What's up with Steph, have you spoken to her, does she know about this?"

"She's coming by Mom's tomorrow. I'm gonna tell her then."

"What about your mom and dad?"

"Tomorrow, I'm gonna talk to everybody tomorrow, but I'm running out of time."

"Bullshit, nothings gonna happen."

"Todd, you don't know what I've been feeling since this guy came to me, the things he's shown me, the way he showed me, I have this power that I don't want. He told me now I'll see what he sees, and all he sees is death. I mean this is his freaking crazy-ass job, this is what he does, I don't know man."

"I got an idea." As Todd said this, the angel appeared outside Jonathan's door. He didn't knock, he didn't enter, he didn't make a sound. Todd continued with his plan.

"Look I'll come by every day and wait for him to show up. When he does, I'll hide in the other room. You let him in, and when you do, I'll come out with this baseball bat and whamo! I take his freaking head off."

"Are you crazy? This guys a freaking angel. He'll tear you apart. Besides, you can't see him anyway, you're not about to die. Only people who are dead or about to die can see and hear him, that's what he said, so just forget it."

"Yeah, yeah, whatever, he comes here I'm swinging for the fences."

The angel heard Todd's plan and, from the other side of the door, stretched out his arm in the direction Todd was standing and sent a flash of heat to attack the entire left side of his body.

Todd shrieked in pain and dropped the baseball bat,

"Ow!"

"What, what happen?" Jonathan asked.

"My hand feels hot ...I suddenly feel hot." Todd stood up touched his forehead with his hand then clutched his chest.

"What's the matter?" Jonathan asked with a concerned look.

"Ughhh," Todd passed out and fell on his back.

"Todd! ...Todd!"

Jonathan checked Todd for a heartbeat. He checked his pulse, he appeared dead, and then the angel came through the wall. Jonathan backed away from him.

"Holy shit, you just walked through that wall, and what the hell did you do to my friend!" he asked angrily.

"Don't worry about him, he'll be fine. Do you see what we mean about you people? The first thing he thought of was violence, if it were in his power to do so, he would have killed me. It never crossed his mind to try and talk it out with me, not that he could've, but a peaceful solution was the last thing he was thinking about, typical of you human beings."

Jonathan shaking his head in a disagreeing manner said, "You're not right; you're just so fucking evil," he replied.

"I'm evil, no son, he took counsel with you to pick up that bat and swing for the fences, he doesn't know who or what I am. I could've been some psychic looking to scam you, but I'm not the scam artist, he believes me to be, because if I were, your friend Todd would've joined the class of the murderers. Don't call me evil. It's you and him that have the evil inside," The angel walked toward the door. "I'm going to leave now. When your friend comes to, tell him I said it won't be for a while, but when his time is near, I promise to visit with him, I will make sure he gets the proper escort, am I understood? You only have six days left." Azraa'el laughed at Jonathan then disappeared.

Jonathan became enraged. Todd started to come back from his unconsciousness rolling around on the floor in agony. Jonathan threw a glass against the wall, frustrated by the angel's taunts, he yelled at his friend.

"Todd, get your ass up. I told you not to fuck with him. Now look what you did; you pissed him off!"

"What happen ...what the hell happen ...awe, I feel sick why do I feel ...?" Unable to get his words out, Todd vomited.

"Great, I warned you, I told you not to mess with him."

"I need a doctor. Somebody help me."

"No, just relax. I'll get some towels and clean this mess up."

"What happen here?" Todd asked.

Jonathan yelled from the back room. "It was the angel. He heard everything you were saying!"

"Oh fuck, I gotta get outta here. This is too weird for me man."

"Here get up on the couch; lay down put this towel on your head, man you don't listen."

"Hey, I was just trying to help you ...fucking angel ...I still don't believe it, I didn't see any angel I didn't see anybody. I gotta get outta this creepy-ass apartment, as soon as my headache goes away."

"I told you he's real."

"Yeah, well, how come nothing happen to you? You look just fine and you were plotting right along with me."

"Hell no! I told you not to do it ...and he gave me a message to give to you."

"Well I don't want to hear it. I don't wanna know anything about this guy, just leave me alone with this crap. I feel sleepy."

Jonathan gave Todd a glass of water, then sat at the end of the couch for two hours contemplating this great being's power and how maybe his fate really is sealed.

"How do I explain this to my family? Their never gonna understand, they're gonna think I'm nuts. "Hi mom, dad, I'm gonna die in six days, nice knowing ya, bye-now, just great. Hey man, are you awake ... Todd ... Todd, [Todd snoring] thanks for your help." Jonathan grabbed a blanket, spread it over Todd, and then made another call to his girlfriend.

"Hello."

"Hi honey."

"Hey."

"Uh, change of plans. Can you meet me at my parent's house tomorrow?"

"I guess, but why do you wanna meet there?"

"Well, I gotta talk to them about something and I just figure you could meet me there."

"I thought we were gonna be alone so that we can talk Jonathan."

"We'll talk, but there some things I have to let everyone know about."

"Hmm ...alright, what time?"

"I'm calling out, so I'm thinking around three or four."

"You know I get out of work at five so I'll be there at six."

"OK, that's fine. I'll see you then."

"OK bye, Jonathan."

After hanging up the phone, he sat on the couch with a puzzled look on his face.

"Hey Todd, ...Todd, wake up. I guess you're spending the night. Jonathan prepared for bed. Tomorrow would be a difficult day.

CHAPTER 11
THE CONFESSION

The alarm clock woke Jonathan at 5:30 a.m. He picked up his phone, dialed the number to his job, and called out sick. He lay in bed going through many scenarios on how to inform his family about what's been going on over the past few days, and what's to come. He got up to check on Todd, but Todd was gone. He left sometime during the middle of the night and left a note.

"Hey man, call me later. I think I'm gonna call out today too, I'm still feeling kinda queasy. I gotta get myself together. Weird shit man, weird shit, talk to you later."

Jonathan glanced around the apartment then walked to the bathroom, ran water in the sink and splashed it over his face; he grabbed his toothbrush and brushed his teeth. His mind was running, mentally he hadn't rested since he met the angel, his physical appearance was a mess, looking almost homeless, needing a shave and a way to get rid of the dark circles under his eyes. He looked in the mirror and stared, he thrust his hand at the glass cracking it, the thought of not being in control of his life overwhelmed him.

He slowly walked back to the living room, feeling sorry for himself, he flopped down on the couch, and after an hour, he snapped his fingers and came up with an idea. "Church! I haven't been there in God knows how long but what the hell. Why didn't I think of this before, a priest, a father, a pastor, somebody has to help me ...yes!"

Jonathan jumped up with renewed energy. He finally came up with a solution, just as he started to run toward the bathroom the phone rang.

"Hello."

"Yeah John, it's Bill."

"Hey Bill."

"Hey. Did you call out today?"

"Uh, yeah I got some family problems to deal with today and I'm gonna try to get in tomorrow."

"Well you know we have deadlines to meet and were gonna need those reports in a couple of days. Tell me you're not gonna hang me out to dry on this."

"No Bill, after I'm done taking care of this problem, I'm gonna work from home and finish up. It's not much left to do. I'm just about done."

"OK, but if you can't finish call me and let me know what you got done and I'll finish it up, OK? Just don't screw me up with this."

"Don't worry, I got it covered. We'll be fine."

"Alright, I'm counting on you."

"I got you covered. I'll call you later."

"Don't forget."

Jonathan ran to the bathroom and took a quick shower, while showering he thought of what church he'd go to; there were a few within blocks from his apartment. "Fuck, I'll go to them all if I have too." After showering he put on a jogging suit and a light jacket, he grabbed his keys and left the apartment. He got downstairs and realized he didn't have a cell phone anymore. He began walking. He stopped at a computer store and bought another one.

He walked three long blocks and ended up at a Catholic church. He walked in and looked around but saw no one. Suddenly a middle-aged nun walked up behind him.

"Can I help you young man?"

Jonathan turned around quickly and greeted her.

"Hello sister," He extended his hand to hers, "I need to speak to a priest."

"There's no one available right now, It's still very early. The priests are in prayer."

"Would there be a problem if I waited? It's very important that I speak to someone."

"Well maybe I can help you. What's your name son?"

"My name is Jonathan."

"And what seems to be your trouble?"

Jonathan took a deep breath wondering how the nun would take what he had to say.

"I've been visited by an angel." Immediately her eyebrows raised in disbelief. "An angel, huh? Well what did this angel say to you?" She grabbed him by the arm and started leading him back out of the church.

"He told me he came to take my soul back to God and that I'm gonna die in ten days, but that was five days ago, and I'm very afraid. Sister I know you probably think I'm a kook, but I'm telling you the truth."

"Well son, why don't you just go back home and lay down for a while and if this angel guy comes to bother you again I want you to call the police and let them take care of it, OK?" He stopped the woman from walking him out of the church and pleaded his case more passionately.

"What? You don't believe me? I'm telling you the truth, please you gotta help me, he's gonna kill me, you have to help me!"

"OK, OK, lower your voice son. Sit here with me. What did you say your name was again?"

"Jonathan, my name is Jonathan Krause."

"OK Jonathan, where did you see this angel?" she asked with disbelief.

"He first came to me while I was at a party."

"A party, what kind of party?"

"It was a business gathering, and the next day he showed up at my apartment and started talking about things in my past that I've never shared with anyone, and he also showed me some of his powers."

"His powers?"

"Yes, as he was talking and had his back turned to me

"I tried to attack him but then he disappeared and reappeared right before my eyes."

She again looked at him with a disbelieving smirk. Staring into his eyes she asked, "At this party were there a lot of drugs around, do you take any drugs?"

Jonathan swallowed, lowering his eyes and looking away he answered bashfully, "Yes, there were, and I did take some stuff that night."

She interrupted him, "Uh, that's what I thought," she threw her hands up in the air and stood up.

"Now listen. We don't have time for games here. You should be ashamed of yourself coming here to waste my time, your time, and the father's time. Chastising him, she pointed her finger in his face,

"Now I want you to get yourself into a program and clean yourself up and come back when you're serious about doing God's work!"

"Sister, I'm very sorry that you think I'm wasting your time, but I'm being honest with you."

"Oh really," she said with sarcasm, "maybe we need to exorcize your house. Maybe you have an evil spirit in your home."

"No. He's not a spirit, he's a man, and he says he works for God and his job is to bring the souls of man back to GOD." She shook her head not believing a word of it.

"Really?"

"Yes."

"OK Jonathan, you'll have to go now," she said, as she again tried to lead him out of the church.

"No, wait. Let me describe him to you," he said anxiously, "he has shoulder length salt-and-pepper hair, a goatee, he's about 5'10, maybe 6 feet, and wear's these weird clothes, kinda like you guys. He said his name is Azraa'el. Now, sister, I'm not leaving here until I see a priest."

The sister sat back down on the bench and just stared at Jonathan for a few seconds. "Um hmm ...wait here, my son."

"OK." Jonathan sat there looking around at the church. The statues and pictures of saints spooked him. He rubbed his hands to keep them from perspiring, he kept glancing anxiously at the door the sister went into, and became impatient.

"What the hell is she doing back there? I've been sitting here for ten minutes," he thought to himself, bouncing his leg up and down. She finally walked back into the seated area. A priest followed her. Jonathan stood up to greet him.

"Hello father," Jonathan extended his hand.

"My son," The priest shook Jonathan's hand.

"I'm Father McCahee. The sister tells me you have an unwanted spirit in your home,"

"No, I said I've been visited by an angel and this angel said I have ten days to live, and then he's gonna take me back to GOD. He said his name is Azraa'el lord over the souls of man." he said with a bit of irritation.

"Are those his words or yours?"

Jonathan looked annoyed. "This is how he introduced himself to me."

"Are you sure son, are you sure he said his name is Azraa'el?"

"Yes .... yes, I know it sounds crazy but this guy."

"Guy, he appeared as a man?" the priest asked.

"Yes, how else is he supposed to appear? He's a man, he's been to my house a couple of times already and told me that in ten days he's bringing me back to the spiritual realm whatever the heck that means. Now, father, please help me. What can I do to stop this?"

The priest looked at the sister; the sister looked at the priest and shrugged her shoulders. The priest put his arm around Jonathan.

"My son, when angels come they normally come to prophets, saints, men of the cloth, you know, religious people. We know you're not a prophet. I haven't heard of any new saints being ordained. Are you a man of the cloth?"

"No but he was very clear about why he came. He came for me, he said he's bringing me back to God in ten days, he said I'm gonna die."

"Did he harm you physically?"

"No."

"And he said he would take you back to the spiritual realm in ten days?"

"Yes. I said it three times already. What are you not understanding? He said I'm gonna die and he's gonna return my soul back to God."

"Jonathan, that being you are describing is commonly known as the angel of death. I believe you may have had a vision of him. Were you sleeping, maybe you were dreaming?"

"No. I wasn't sleeping, I didn't have a dream, and it wasn't some vague vision. I saw him at a party, and, after that, he showed up at my house twice. I saw him and we spoke. I'm not making this up."

"OK, but it's strange. The book never mentions this angel interacting with people who are still alive. He never hurt you and he only speaks of spiritual things? My question is why do you think you saw the angel of death?"

"I don't think I saw him, I know I saw him. There are some things in my past that he mentioned to me, and I think that's why he's here for me."

"What things, son?"

"I haven't been the best person I can be. I did some really bad things a long time ago, and he knows all about it."

"Do you wish to make confession?"

Jonathan thought for a second. "I'm not a Catholic."

"It's OK. We're all God's children no matter what religion race, creed, or color."

"And this angel has been speaking to my conscious, telling me to confess."

"God forgives all," the priest replied.

Jonathan sat quietly again, contemplating his sins. They all sat quietly for a few seconds the priest said a prayer, and Jonathan began his confession.

"Back when I lived in Kansas, I stole my neighbors' dog, a white miniature poodle. They looked all over the neighborhood for their dog, but I had him. I kept him for five days."

"Why did you take the dog, Jonathan?"

"Because I hated the way they played with him out in the yard. They just loved and enjoyed that dog so much, and I guess I just didn't like seeing them so happy, so I took him, to see how they would feel then. I had him tied up in an old abandon barn. I would go to the local store and steel cans of dog food to feed him. After three days, they posted a reward for him, five-hundred dollars, and of course, I returned the dog and got the reward money. I told them I found him in the park. They didn't care where I found him, they were so happy just to have him back; they gave me the money in cash. I thought I was rich, most money I'd ever seen, my mom and dad took it from me though and put it away, but I think they used some of it to pay bills because all I ever saw was about half of it. I bought a bike that cost a hundred seventy-five dollars, and a couple of pairs of pants my mom made me buy, and they cost thirty bucks a piece. So where'd the other two and change go? Yeah, I kept track of the money, I really didn't care though, I had a shiny new bike."

"Continue, my son."

"Well not too long ago, a few years back, I slipped a pill in a girl's drink so I could have sex with her. I probably didn't have to do that because I think she would have had sex with me any way. It was obvious she liked me, but I never gave her the chance to decide. I kind of helped her make the decision. I'm a scum bag, father. I deserve to rot in hell."

"You are cleansing your soul. God will forgive you."

"With my luck, they'll have a special place for me to burn right next to freaking Hitler."

"I've heard worst confessions, Jonathan."

"Yeah, well, there's something else."

"OK," the father said with anticipation

"About five years ago, when I first became a broker, I got a call from a friend who knew of an older couple that were looking to do a small investment, not a lot, just a small investment for about ten thousand dollars. They were trying to buy some stocks for their granddaughter. It was supposed be a birthday present for her. The investment did pretty good, so I convinced them to buy more stocks, diversify, invest bigger, for more money. Long story short, I ended up stealing over one-hundred-thousand dollars from them. I became the wonder boy at my firm, well at least for the moment I was, and that old couple well they got the shaft. After their first couple of investments did well, I sold them some dead-dog stocks; they lost a bundle, they kept trying to catch lightening in a bottle twice, and I kept egging them on to invest more. They just kept writing me checks. Their money helped me get my place downtown, it helped me get somewhat noticed at work—yeah, I'm having a great life off someone else's hard work, and elderly people no less. Now how can God forgive someone like me? I know this is why the angel is coming for me. He say's my time is up, I don't want to die, father, help me."

"Is that it Jonathan, is that all you want to confess?" The priest blessed Jonathan and made the sign of the cross over his head. He stared at the priest feeling paranoid. He felt that the priest knew his thoughts. He wanted to talk to him about his old friend Jimmy, but he just stared at the priest. The priest smiled at him.

Jonathan answered, "No, that's it, father."

"OK, I will pray for you, now you must go home and pray as well, if what your saying is true about this spirit, there is nothing that can be done to prevent this. The angel is carrying out God's plan. No one can stop it. You have confessed your sins and cleansed your soul. God will forgive you, have faith, my son. But honestly, this seems like it's just a figment of your imagination. The sister told me about your using drugs." the priest shook his head and waved his finger at Jonathan in a disapproving manner.

"Have faith? Is that your solution to my problem? Oh, I see what this is, you don't believe me? You think I'm lying about the angel. I confess, pour my heart out to you and for what, for you to patronize me and take me for a joke! Fine, I don't even know why I bothered. I'm getting the hell out of here. You should have your collar taken away from you because you were no help at all." Jonathan stood and walked up the aisle and walked toward the doors.

"I'm sorry, Jonathan," the priest said.

"Thanks father, thanks for nothing." Jonathan stormed out of the church.

CHAPTER 12
WUSU'S STORY

Rafiqiel was on a mission to retrieve the soul of the lion; again, he appeared as a lion, this time twice the size of Wusu. He roared in order to provoke him into coming to investigate. Wusu, always ready for war, did exactly that, he charged running toward the sound of the other lion. Wusu spotted the intruder and stopped suddenly, he was surprised by the size of the other lion, Rafiqiel roared. Wusu roared back, and the angel understood him.

"You present yourself as a lion in order to bring fear to me and my clan, but I know it is you, Rafiqiel. Now come forward and be as you are."

Rafiqiel revealed himself as the spiritual being and laughed.

"Forgive me, young warrior, this is my idea of a joke." Rafiqiel rubbed the lions head to comfort him.

"Come walk with me Rafiqiel. I will show you my land. Look to your left, there is the place where, when I was only four years old, I slew the great lion before me. He had gotten old. I and two others like me, we desired his position, so we plotted an attack, but he was a skillful warrior, and, as we plotted, he perceived the danger and moved his family five miles away from where he lived. At first, we were confused as to where to find him, but we tracked his scent, and his territory was great, so five miles meant he was still king of the region. By the end of the day, we had found his family, and we attempted to take the females, but they resisted our advances and fought us. We were cautious with them, for the walking all day made us weary, and there was no sign of the old lion, so we stayed clear until the light of day had gone by, and we slept.

The old lion was sharp, a ferocious killer, and, while we slept, he attacked and pounced down upon us, and, with a swipe of his paw, he gashed the throat of one of my companions, killing him instantly. The weight of the old lion was twice what I am. His weight alone instilled fear in us, but we had to fight. As he sank his teeth into the other lion that walked with me, I attacked him from behind, but he didn't focus on me, he had his mind on the other. My comrade put up a good fight, but the old lion knew well how to kill, and, after two minutes, my friends were gone. Soon fear had replaced my bravery. The old lion had now turned to do battle with me, and I perceived his weariness, but the old warrior was ready to defend his ten-mile territory.

He stood still and let out a great roar. I backed up as he moved toward me, by then I was convinced his strength was unmatched. 'I was ready to retreat, but, ah, I see blood coming from his hind leg where I attacked him from behind, and now I have renewed confidence, my energy is soaring. We lunged at each other and while we battled, I tell him, you are old and I am young, he roared in protest. I tell him, you have a wound on the back of your leg, you will die today, but it seemed the old lion battled harder, but I also battled harder. I say to him, you have battled three lions today, two of them you killed, but you will not kill me, you are old and tired. I lunged at his throat and swiped at his bloody hind leg. Suddenly, the battle came to a complete stop. We stared at each other, and the old lion turned and walked a short distance and collapsed. I stayed and watched him for a while, to make sure he did not get up again. Sometime went by, and then he let out one last moan. I knew then that he was finished, and I left the old lion for the birds that eat the dead. I went back to his family and stood before them to inform them that the old king was dead, I did battle with him and I killed him, and now I am the great warrior lion Wusu, the king."

The old lion had three lionesses in his family and five cubs, two male and three females. One of the males I caused to die; the other I chased away. There could only be one king. I quickly took control of the lioness and made known fast in that region that I was the new king. I attacked any four-legged creature that came too close. I went about spraying my scent on as much land as I could, and I roared to send a message that I battled the great one and defeated him. I had no fear or respect for any four-footed creature, I am Wusu, and this entire region is mine.

I stood to listen for any sound of protest, but none dared. four moon cycles had gone by and the three lionesses brought forth two cubs each of my own seed, four males two female. After that, I brought my clan back to the territory where I was born, so that my kingship would be known in all directions. Look at the other beast, Rafiqiel, when I walk through, they scatter, be it buffalo, elephant or lion, none dare challenge me. Growing up, there were many in my clan, my father was a great warrior, but he was not as skilled as my mother, she possessed great power, and I watched her do battle many times, and her skill was unmatched.

I'm sure I get most of my strength and bravery from her, not that my father was incapable of fierce battle, but my mother challenged even full adult males. And neither was my mother nor father killed; they are still living in the upper part of this region, where I'm sure they have heard the roar of their son as the new king.

Wusu walked with the angel and talked for hours about his legendary youth, as the sun began to set on the African plain.

"This is my favorite time of the day Rafiqiel; the heat will subside, and the breeze brushes against my mane, it's very calm at this time." Rafiqiel smiled at the young lion.

"Rafiqiel, you are a terrible guest."

"What do you mean, my friend?" the angel asked.

"We have been together the whole day, and you have not spoken a word, why is that?"

"Because, Wusu, your time is up."

Rafiqiel levitated thirty feet up into a tree. Wusu looked up, confused by the angel's action, and while his attention was on the angel, hunters shot down the great warrior lion for the sake of making his skin for sale. As they hoisted the lion's body on to a vehicle, the angel extracted his essence, and spoke to his spirit.

"It was never the four-footed creatures you had to fear, Wusu. Now come with me, my friend. I will show you a place where you will have no need to defend or attack. Because you enjoy being a warrior and a king, we will place you in the realm of the four-footed creatures, and they will help you to exist in peace."

CHAPTER 13

MOM AND DAD

Jonathan sat for hours thinking of how to explain his situation to his mother and father.

He arrived at their home around five o'clock p.m. and stood outside the door, hesitant to ring the doorbell, he pulled out his cell phone and called Todd.

"Hello."

"Eh, Todd, what are you doing?"

"What's up, Jonathan. I'm still trying to recover from whatever the hell happened at your apartment."

"OK, but I need you to come over to my parent's house like as soon as possible, I'm already here."

"What for?"

"I gotta tell my family what's going on with this angel stuff, and I need some support. You know there never gonna believe me. Plus, I'm gonna tell them what happen when I was a kid."

"When you were a kid, what happen when you were a kid?"

"It's hard to explain on the phone, so I need you to come to my mom and dad's, like now," he said as he paced outside the door.

"Aw man, I don't really wanna be there for that dude; I mean that's something you should do on your own, between you and your family, ya know, and, besides, I don't feel well."

"Yeah, I hear you, but I'm having a tough enough time dealing with this on my own, besides you're like family anyway, so just do this for me. Get yourself together and meet me over here, OK?"

Todd was silent for a minute.

"Alright, give me an hour."

"Thanks man."

Jonathan's father, heard him on the phone outside, and opened the door.

"Hey, son, how long you been out here!" They hugged each other.

"Oh, hi, Dad—Hey, Todd I'll see you when you get here— How's everything, Dad?"

"I'm fine. It's you we're worried about. Come on in," Jonathan's mom met him at the door.

"Jonathan! Hello, son, you look well. How are you doing?" she said as they embraced.

"I'm fine, Mom."

"How's work? How's, Stephanie?"

"Work is fine; Steph is coming over after work."

"Here?" she asked, surprised.

"Yeah, and Todd's coming too. Hey, did you guys get in touch with Jen? She should be here also."

"Alright son, now what's the big powwow for, what's going on?"

"Dad, I just wanna wait for everyone to be here and then I can talk to everybody at once, OK? So let's just talk about something else, what's new, what have you and Mom been up to?"

Jonathan's parents are church going people, and to tell them he's been visited by an angel would be hard for them to accept; he was never one for spirituality. Dad is a retired warehouse foreman from a major distribution company, and Mom became a homemaker after working as a secretary for five years at the same place. Both in their mid-fifties they moved the family from Kansas to New York City shortly after the incidences Jonathan had been involved in, in his old neighborhood.

The move from Kansas was a plan to help Jonathan out of his mild depression. They never knew that it was he who was totally responsible for the incident involving him, Mikey, and Jimmy; they tried to comfort him as much as possible during that time. The depression is something Jonathan blocked out of his memory, and he doesn't recall ever being in that state of mind.

He sat and talked with his father about everything from sports to politics, this comforted him, and he even laughed at times, something he hadn't been able to do for the past few days. He seemed to forget his troubles, at least for an hour; Jonathan's mom looked in on the two men every few minutes while preparing dinner for the family. She moved around in a nervous state most of the evening, she could sense Jonathan was bringing bad news and couldn't help but feel anxious. The doorbell rang, his mom yelled out, "I'll get it!

Todd and Stephanie had arrived together.

"Hello, it's good to see you two!"

"Hello, Mrs. Krause." Stephanie said.

"Now, now, you know we agreed you would call me mom, Stephanie, you and Jonathan are going to be married soon, right? She said as she kissed Stephanie on the cheek.

"Right, I'm sorry ... Mom."

Jonathan stood up to meet his girlfriend and tried to kiss her on the lips, but she turned her head and gave him her cheek, still angry about last weekend, she wasn't so ready to forgive him. He grabbed her by the hand and led her into the dining room.

"Honey, are you still angry with me?" he asked.

"I just don't understand why we had to meet here. We're supposed to be alone so you can explain your recent childish behavior, what's this all about Jonathan?"

He faced her and stroked her hair before speaking.

"Remember what I told you the other day, well it's true, and I'm really going to..."

His mom interrupted, "Jens on her way; she's five minutes from the house."

"I'm going to explain everything tonight," Jonathan said.

"Are you on that I'm-gonna-die kick again? Oh please, Jonathan, I hope this is not why you called me here."

She walked away, back to the living room, staring at him with disgust. Todd came over to comfort him; he patted Jonathan on the back.

"Man, suck's to be you right now, huh?"

"Thanks Todd, you always know just what to say."

"I'm just kidding dude, relax."

Jonathan's sister Jennifer walked in.

"Hello, hello, hello."

"Hey! Jen's here, now we can eat." Their father said. The family greeted Jennifer. Then, they gathered in the dining room for dinner. They ate and talked for about an hour, everyone giving up dates about what's going on in their lives. After Todd gave his day-to-day routine, the room became awkwardly silent, and Jonathan's father broke it.

"Well, Jonathan, we're all here, so what gives?"

Jonathan paused and looked around the table.

"Well everything at work is great." his father pressured him.

"No, no, no, I mean why this big powwow; now c'mon, son, give it to us straight." Jonathan paused again.

"Well a few days ago, I was out with Todd at a party at our boss's house on Long Island, and ... an angel appeared to me."

Everyone at the table sat quietly and stared at Jonathan with curiosity.

His father spoke first, "What ...what do ya mean, angel?"

"Alright, this guy came to me and says he an angel, how he's responsible for the souls of man and that when people die he brings their soul back to God, back to heaven, and in ten days he's coming for my soul, he's bringing me back to God. He came to me five days ago, so what I'm saying Mom, Dad, Jen ... I only have a few days left to live. His mom put her hand to her head.

"Oh, Jonathan what are you talking about?" she asked sarcastically with a giggle.

"Aaargh, is this the big revelation?" his dad asked.

"I know it sounds crazy, but this is real. The guy is real. He knew all about me, he knew things no one else knew about me. I've seen and felt his power, and this guy, this being, is the real deal."

"You honestly want us to believe an angel came and spoke to you?"

"Yeah Dad, hey, ask Todd. He got a little taste of the angel's power, tell him Todd."

"Sir, I didn't believe this story either, but when Jonathan told me the guy showed up at his apartment, I wanted to be there so we could take care of him, as I'm telling Jonathan what I was gonna do to this "angel," all of a sudden I get a hot flash shoot through the whole left side of my body; it burned like hell. Now I don't know what it was, but whatever it was, it knocked me flat on my back. I was out cold for I don't know how long, and when I finally came to, 'I was in pain, I felt nauseous, I didn't know where 'I was at, and I have been feeling uneasy ever since. Jonathan warned me not to go after the guy. Now I'm not saying it was an angel, because I never saw him, I'm just saying it was really weird."

"Well I think your both nuts. Hey, no offense, but why you? Why would an angel come and talk to you?" Jonathan stared at his father then looked at his mom; he walked over to her and held her hand.

"Do you know how I became so successful at work?"

"We all know what you do for a living son," she said with a smile.

"Yeah but you don't know how I became well off so fast."

"What did you do Jonathan?" Dad asked sternly. Jonathan put his head down in shame.

"I swindled half a million dollars from an elderly couple."

Jonathan's mother let out a gasp and put her hand over her mouth.

"It was a few elderly couples, I got so good at getting money from older people I became the Wall Street whiz kid."

"Oh, that's just terrible. Why would you do that?"

"Your mother is right. You should turn some of that money over to charity and beg God for forgiveness. Is this why your angel came to talk to you? Aaah, I'm still not convinced," his dad started reaching for the food placed around the table.

"I know it's hard to believe, Dad, but there's something else."

"Yeah what else you wanna hit us with," he said looking at his wife with a wink and a smile.

"Do you guys remember Jimmy Benton?"

"How could we forget him?"

"Do you remember Michael Pratsky?"

"Yeah, the other hooligan you use to run around with back then, what about em?" his dad asked.

"Well ...you remember what happen to Jimmy?"

All eyes were on Jonathan, his mom got up out of her chair looking terrified, like she knew what he was trying to say. His dad got up out of his chair and walked over to him and put both hands on Jonathan's shoulder's. They looked each other in the face.

"What are you talking about, son, what are you trying to say?" his father asked.

"It ...it was me." His mom gasped.

"It was you what?" asked his father.

"It was me and Mikey."

"It was you and Mikey what!" his dad demanded.

"Me and Mikey ...We killed Jimmy."

Jonathan's mom ran into the bedroom crying. His sister, who, being five years younger, never knew of the tragic event, stood with Stephanie in disbelief with shocked looks on their faces. Todd sat at the table staring at his best friend.

"You did what ... you killed that little boy! No, no, he drowned swimming in the lake; they found him in the water!"

"Dad ... we threw him in the water," Jonathan said somberly. "We were playing around up on the mountain, and me and Mikey thought it would be fun to throw him into the lake. I grabbed his hands, Mikey grabbed his legs, and we swung him off the cliff into the water. We thought he would make it, we were just kidding around, we never intended for that to happen. We were scared out of our minds, but all we could do was watch him try to stay afloat ... We couldn't help him, we knew we did something wrong, we were just so afraid. We watched him go under, and then we stood on the mountain for hours. Mikey cried his eyes out, and he started blaming me. I guess he was right, but we vowed never to say a word about what really happen."

Jonathan's dad grabbed him by the shirt angrily and pushed him up against the dining room wall. "You thought it would be fun! You thought it would be fun to throw a twelve-year-old kid off a three-hundred-foot cliff to his death? The whole community was out searching for this kid until they found him washed up on the rocks three miles away. You let everyone believe that he just drowned. I don't believe this; a kid dies because you and that little bastard Mikey thought it would be fun? We told you to stay away from that punk!"

Todd walked over and broke the two men apart.

"Calm down, Mr. Krause."

"And Mikey's ... dead."

"What"! His dad yelled.

"Mikey died in a car accident, two years after Jimmy."

"My God ... how do you know that, are you still in contact with these people!" Dad asked.

"No."

"Well how the hell do you know he died?"

"The angel told me."

Jonathan's mother could be heard still crying in the bedroom. A look of disgust came over Stephanie's face, and his father continued ranting.

"Look, I don't know what the hell is going on, but this is nuts. I don't even understand what you're talking about. This isn't news, this is a nightmare. Are you serious! You know people always thought you had something to do with that boy's death. For a whole year, I would hear little rumors, people staring when they saw us out in the street, but we brushed it off, we thought they just wanted someone to blame, but they were right the whole time. I don't believe it. Do you hear your mother in there?" Dad faced Jonathan.

"Why did you bring the whole family here for this, did you come here to break mine and your mother's heart, because that's what you're doing." His dad slammed his fist down on the table.

"I'm sorry, Dad. I knew this would be hard for everyone, but I have to tell the truth about what happen before the angel comes for me."

Stephanie walked over to Jonathan, she spoke softly to him, "Please don't call me anymore." She grabbed her coat and ran out of the house. Jennifer went after her hoping to get her to stay.

"Look, look what you've done, you ruined everything now!" His dad said.

Jonathan's mother came out of the bedroom. "Do his parents know?" she asked drying her eyes with tissue.

"No, Mom, but I'd like to tell them."

His dad objected. "No! It's bad enough they had to go through something like that to begin with, they've probably never gotten over it, and to have you come back after all these years and drop this on them, it wouldn't be right nor would it do any good."

"But, Dad, the angel is in my head telling me to clear my conscious, to clear my soul, and I think Jimmy's family should know."

"I'm asking you as your father, please don't tell this kid's parents about this, don't go pour salt on an old wound that may still be open, don't do it. The whole town was torn apart by this thing–the media coverage, the newspaper articles, the community was the focal point of the state. It was a three-ring circus; we couldn't get a moment's peace. All those days sitting with the kid's parents, trying to console them, and the whole time you and Mikey knew what happen?" His dad looked to the ceiling clenching his fist in frustration. "Unbelievable," he shouted.

Jonathan's sister reentered the house. "She's gone Jonathan; she said she never wants to see you again."

Jonathan lowered his head and breathed in and out deeply, figuring that would-be Stephanie's reaction, yet still disappointed by it.

"Well, what do we do now?" his mom asked.

"We're gonna do nothing, we're gonna say nothing," his dad replied.

"No, James, we can't just keep quiet now that we know what happen," his mom said with teary eyes. "That's exactly what were gonna do. If we say anything to anybody about this, it'll do no good, not to mention the fact Jonathan could still be prosecuted for this. There's no statute of limitation on killing a person. Do you want our son to go to jail, Alice?" She shook her head no; he turned to his son and asked. "Is that what you want, Jonathan?"

Jonathan thought for a few seconds.

"It really doesn't matter Dad. I told you earlier, I'm not gonna be around much longer; the angel is coming for me."

"Awh come on already with this angel stuff! Alright, who are you the pope? Angels don't come to regular guys. Now cut the nonsense out. You got it off your chest, now just leave it alone!"

Jonathan and his mom and dad sat in the living room for two hours discussing the entirety of what happen during that time of his childhood, while Todd and Jonathan's sister Jenny played cards in the dining room, trying hard to eavesdrop. It was 10:30 p.m. Jonathan stood up and slowly walked to the dining room and asked Todd, "Are you ready?"

His mother walked over and stood next to the two men. She grabbed Jonathan's hand.

"Son, you know we love you, and we'll always be here for you, we're your parents. You can come and talk to us anytime about whatever's bothering you." Still crying, she hugged him and kissed his cheek.

"I know, Mom ... it's getting late. I think I better go."

"Why don't you stay a few days with us, you and Jen. I think we need to talk about this. It's a terrible thing what happen with this kid. You held this in all this time; it must have been tearing you up inside?" Jonathan looked around the room remembering his childhood; with half a smile, he took a deep breath.

"No, I better go, I gotta see my doctor tomorrow to get the results from my physical."

His sister brought their coats to them. She handed Jonathan his. He hugged her, and she whispered she would call him tomorrow. Todd said good-bye to the Krause's and walked toward the door. Jonathan kissed his mom. He shook his dad's hand, pulled him in close, and hugged him.

He walked to the door turned and looked at his family as tears formed in his eyes, he said good-bye to them, with thoughts that he might not ever see them again, and walked out of the house. The two friends walked to the subway and caught a train. They sat silently, exhausted from the emotional evening. Jonathan sat with his head tilted back staring at the ceiling of the train.

"So what was the kid like Jonathan? I mean, what happen? Why'd you do that?"

Jonathan sat up teary eyed and spoke about the event.

"It was three of us, me, Mikey, and Jimmy, we were all friends, but Jimmy was the wimp out of the three, always whining, blond hair a little freckled-face chubby kid, he always had to be in before it got dark. We used to mess with him all the time. Me and Mikey hung out a lot. My parents hated him. They didn't like me being around him, but he used to crack me up you know, always getting into shit. He was the neighborhood bad kid, I mean as far as the adults were concerned, he was a real smartass.

We used to horse around on this mountain. The mountain had a three-hundred-foot drop with a river about 20-30 feet deep below, and a trail that ran parallel to the edge of it—one slip, man, and down you go. I remember it like it happen yesterday.

One day we're up there just walking around through the woods and we hit the trail, I whispered to Mikey to let Jimmy walk up ahead, so he's walking along talking about what his mom was cooking for dinner and how he and his family were going away for the summer. As he's talking, Mikey tackled and grabbed him by the feet and he started dragging him. Jimmy's screaming No! No! Stop. He's got dirt and shit going all down his pants. Mikey tells me to grab his hands. Now I got his hands, and Mikey's got his feet. Jimmy's twisting and turning trying to get loose, still screaming at the top of his lungs, me and Mikey, the whole time laughing our asses off," Jonathan says with a smile.

"We dragged him closer to the edge of the cliff and start to swing him back and forth, now he's crying but we didn't care. We count 1, 2, 3, and we threw him off the cliff into the river. On his way down, I knew immediately it was bad. You should have seen him flailing around screaming. I knew we really messed up ... We never thought he would drown ... We weren't trying to kill him, we were kids, we were just horsing around, we didn't mean for him to die."

"Damn Jonathan how old was the kid?"

"He was the same age as us, twelve."

Todd shook his head in disbelief.

"Wow, who da thought, that's a pretty fucked up story."

"Yeah, I know that Todd, thanks for reminding me."

"I'm just saying man it's kinda wild, so what happen after the kid died, did you guys get arrested, go to jail?"

"No, the police thought he just fell in and drowned, a lot of us kids use to play up there, but we weren't supposed too. Parents always thought something like that would happen. I stayed in the house for days just thinking what we done. The night it happened he didn't come home, his parents called the cops and they looked for him that night.

The cops thought maybe he just ran away for a while, but, after the second day, when he didn't show up, they started thinking he might have been kidnapped. They went house to house checking basements and attics. It was crazy, but Me and Mike kept our mouths shut even though we felt terrible about it. We were more afraid of getting in trouble so we said nothing, not even to each other, we didn't talk about it."

"So you guys got away with it."

"If you wanna see it that way, but I think about that day all the time, I don't think I got away with anything. It haunts me to this day. But I think this is why this guy is after me, I've done some really fucked up shit in my life, and now I'm gonna pay for it."

"So what else did you do? You know what, never mind, I don't wanna know. I'm here for you though."

The two friends sat in silence for fifteen minutes; Todd, imagining what his friend was feeling, offered words of comfort.

"Well everybody knows now, right? That's what you wanted to do, let your family know the secrets of your past? You did good, you did the right thing."

"Yeah, but they don't believe me. They think I'm lying about the angel. They think I'm full of shit, and Steph, Steph is gone," he looked at Todd and pointed to his watch. "Twelve o'clock, just four days left," he closed his eyes and slept the whole ride home.

CHAPTER 14
THE RESULTS

With four days passed, Jonathan tossed and turned throughout the night, thoughts of the angel, his parents, the idea that his days are possibly numbered, interrupted his sleep. He rose from his bed at his normal time, made a call to his job, and spoke with his supervisor.

"Hey, uh Bill, good morning, uh, I'm not gonna make it in today, still going through ..."

"Look, Jonathan, if you don't get me those invoices today, don't bother coming back. You promised me you wouldn't jam me up. I'm not gonna wait another day for you to get your act together. In the meantime, call for a courier and send me those reports today or that's it, you're finished."

His supervisor hung up the phone. Jonathan thought for a minute. He put on a pot of coffee and then walked into the bathroom to get ready for another trying day. Ten minutes later, he walked out of the bathroom. As he sat down to watch the morning news, he noticed the answering machine flashing and he pressed play.

"Hello ... this is Dr. Bashir. I'm calling for Jonathan Krause. Jonathan, you can come to the hospital to discuss the results of your physical exam. Come to St. Vincent's on Twenty-Third Street. My office is being painted so I'm seeing all of my patients at the hospital, OK? So, between one o'clock and two I'll see you then." For Jonathan, one o'clock couldn't come soon enough. Since interacting with the angel, it was hard to keep his mind focused on one specific thing for very long. He sat down at his computer anyway to finish the reports his supervisor now demanded, not for fear of losing his job but merely to pass the time.

Soon after he started, he picked up the phone and dialed Stephanie's number, and to his surprise, she answered, but the second she heard his voice she hung up. He redialed and got her answering machine and left an apologetic message.

For at least a year, his behavior as far as their relationship goes, had become increasingly intolerable for her, and now the revelation of his past was too much for her to bear. She endured Jonathan's cheating and drug escapades and had given him plenty of opportunity to change the course of his life. His stubbornness was descriptive of who he is and why she felt the need to leave him, and this latest incident made it easy for her to do it. Not believing his story about an angel and having a few days left to live, she felt certain it was he who sealed the end of their relationship.

Jonathan worked for two hours and managed to finish the reports. He glanced over at the clock, which now said 10:00 a.m., he went to the kitchen and made himself breakfast. As he sat down to eat, he contemplated what he should do for the next two hours before going to see the doctor.

He looked around the huge apartment, an old storage building converted into extremely large living quarters, too much for one person. He loved the spaciousness of the place, but sitting there, he felt very alone. He looked through a photo album filled with pictures of himself, Stephanie, and many of his closest friends, and it made him happy and sad at the same time. He reminisced about better times and thought how it might all be over. He closed the album and finished his breakfast. The telephone rang, and he picked it up.

"Hello."

"Eh man, you OK?"

"What's up, Todd? Yeah, I'm OK."

"I guess you took off from work?"

"Yeah, I gotta see the doctor today."

"Right, right, you did tell me that."

"Hey, take a ride with me."

"Well, I'm at work now. What time do you have to be there?"

"I'm going at one."

"OK, I'll have to call you back; I'll let you know by eleven thirty."

"OK, because I'm gonna leave here by twelve."

"Alright, I'll let you know by then, talk to you later."

"OK, talk to you later."

Jonathan called his job to have a messenger pick up the reports, he felt good, He could at least keep his word to his supervisor and finish the work. He glanced over at the clock and walked around the apartment pacing, unable to sit still, he looked for something to do, but there was nothing to do. He looked in the hallway closet and grabbed a golf club he liked to practice swinging while in the apartment.

He swung the club for ten minutes and then placed it back in its bag. Then came across an old hand ball; he picked it up gripping it in his hand, he stared at it, and thought back to his high school days when the daily exercise was handball, a game Jonathan loved to play. He walked around the apartment bouncing the ball and slapping it against the wall; he tossed it around for twenty minutes, and then sat down on the floor and thought about Stephanie.

"How could she leave me? Why now, that's OK if the doctor gives me a clean bill of health, to hell with her for good ...I can't believe she just walked out on me like that, damn it!"

Jonathan ranted alone and aloud about how his life had turned upside down, he went through a wide range of emotions, from optimism to pessimism, and he kept glancing over at the clock on the wall, as he talked to himself.

He picked himself up off the floor, pulled out his wallet, and threw away all unnecessary business cards and phone numbers, and thought to himself, "I'll be fine, I'm gonna be OK."

With an hour until he leaves for the hospital, Jonathan stood in front of the television and browsed through the channels. He came across a body fitness show and started doing jumping jacks. A minute into the session he began laughing hysterically at himself and quit the exercise.

He put on the stereo and played music. He raised the volume as loud as he could and sang along with his favorite band, he listened to a few selections and then turned the music off. He walked over to the telephone and stared at it, hoping it would ring and it would be Stephanie on the other end. He sat at the edge of the couch rocking back and forth nervously. 'At 11:30 a.m., he grabbed a cup of coffee, walked over to the door and picked up his morning newspaper. He sat down to read it and then the phone rang.

"Hello."

"Eh dude, it's me."

"Hey, what's up Todd, are you gonna go or what?"

"Yeah, but I'm gonna have to meet you down there. I'm in a meeting as we speak, looks like I'm gonna be here another hour. So as soon as I'm done, I'll just walk over."

"Alright, good, I should be leaving here in another ten minutes so I'll see you down there. Just call me on my cell so we don't miss each other. I'll see you later."

"OK." Jonathan sat a little while longer reading his paper and drinking his coffee, he glanced at the clock and noticed it was time to leave; he looked around hastily for his keys then grabbed them off the table and walked quickly toward the door. He looked in the mirror before leaving, then ran back to the bathroom grabbed a brush and did a few strokes on his hair; he splashed on some cologne and again walked toward the door, he stepped out into the hall, turned and looked around the apartment then closed the door and left.

Jonathan took the stairs to the ground floor; he walked a block or two and then caught a cab. The ride over was nerve racking, traffic blocked many of the streets; he arrived at the hospital a half hour late. He hurried out of the cab, ran into the building, and went straight to the receptionist.

"Hi, I'm here to see Dr. Bashir," The nurse called up to the floor the doctor was working on.

"Sir, the doctor is on the fifth floor, when you go up, see the nurse at the nurse's station and ask for him."

Jonathan thanked the nurse and as he walked to the elevator the angel appeared, he kept himself in the ethereal form so Jonathan would not see him. Jonathan boarded the elevator, and the angel followed him on. As they rode up, the doors opened at every floor, with no one boarding: first, second, third. On the fourth floor, the doors opened again. No one boarded the elevator, but a voice was heard calling.

"Azraa'el.

The angel immediately got off, and followed the voice.

"Azraa'el, I'm over here."

The angel looked around and saw only infants, as he roamed the maternity ward, all cried the cry of the newly born. A young woman stood just outside the ward leaning against a glass window staring at the newborns. Azraa'el walked by her. He glanced at her for a few seconds and knew her fate. None of the babies saw the angel, none except one, but he did not cry out like the others. The angel approached the infant and greeted him.

"Peace be upon you, Elam. Why have you called out to me?" The infant spoke with the voice of a three-year-old child.

"PEACE to you, Lord Azraa'el. Look at the woman on the other side of the window."

"I see her."

"She's my mother, listen to her Azraa'el."

The woman began to speak to the infant from the other side of the glass. "I'm always going to love you, we found your name in a special book, and you are a special child, your name will be Elam, and we will be together always. You made me complete. We are family now. I'll never leave you alone. We'll be together forever."

The angel acknowledged the woman and confirmed her words to the infant.

"She loves you as a mother should love her child."

"Yes, my Lord, but she is of those who will return to the Most High tonight."

"I'm aware, but she will leave with one of my legion, not with me."

"You have heard her words my Lord, as her time is near, so is mine. My mission on this realm was to be born and make my mother's life complete. Before I came here, she felt incomplete in her heart and mind, she believed women should bring forth children to complete their womanhood, but you and I know that is far from the truth. The Most High held back her womb so that I would be born to her, that she would not die from any other pregnancy and that I would be the one to fulfill her life and make her feel complete. Now, she has promised me we will be together forever and we will be a family, and she says she will never leave me. As you know, my physical life will end later in the evening; my mother's life will also end. I ask that you let her keep her promise to me and allow me to bring her back to the spirit realm."

The angel looked upon the young soul with admiration and smiled at him. "You are a young spirit to travel such a distance alone, you would be responsible not only for your soul but hers also, and, besides, I have not been informed of what you ask of me, for something like this, permission must come from the Most High."

"I have just come from the upper realm, my lord, I know the way back, before my physical birth I spoke with your brothers Michael and Gabriel about returning with my mother. They did speak on my behalf to the Supreme Ruler, and the Supreme Ruler has left this decision in your hands."

Azraa'el paused and closed his eyes as if he were getting a message from a far-off distance, and then he decreed.

"By the power of the Most High, what you have asked will be permitted, return on the path that runs between the sun and the moon, which is before the day takes over night or the night takes over day, find the middle path my son, and may peace and blessing be upon you."

"May peace be upon you, Azraa'el, lord of souls, today tomorrow and forever."

Elam the infant smiled at the woman on the other side of the window and then watched as Azraa'el hovered over him for a moment and then slowly vanish. As soon as the lord of souls was out of sight, the infant became as the other newborns in the ward and began to cry out. Immediately, the physical world is an irritation to them and so they cry. Later that evening, the mother of Elam thought to be sleeping after the exhausting labor, lay in her bed hemorrhaging for more than an hour.

By design, the hospital staff was neglectful of her, but the plan of the Creator will be done, so as result of a rough delivery, her life was over at 6:00 p.m. Elam, her son and escort, stopped breathing at 5:58 p.m., and finished his life at 6:00 p.m. also.

Jonathan sat in the lounge area of the hospital nervously waiting for a half hour. Finally, the doctor walked over to him with his chart.

"Jonathan, buddy, how are you today?"

"Hey doc, I'm fine ... I hope."

"Come on let's talk over by the nurse's station." Azraa'el showed up immediately, still unseen, and listened to what the doctor had to say.

"Well, we have all of the test results back, and I'm happy to say you're in top physical condition."

"Whew, yes!" Jonathan exclaimed.

"Your EKG is fine, your cholesterol is good, all the test came back negative, you have no 'STD's, your blood pressure was a little elevated, not too bad—probably from the stress—but other than that you're in great shape."

"Yes! So, I'm fine, right doc, I'm not gonna die?"

"We will all die someday, the doctor said smiling, but you ...not today, you're in great shape, take it easy with that stuff and you should be fine, OK."

"You got it doc ,I'm taking it easy, whew I feel great!"

"OK, Jonathan, have a great day."

"Thank you doc, thank you so much."

Jonathan shook the doctor's hand and walked back toward the elevators. He waited with a smile on his face, clapping his hands, he boarded the elevator and took it to the lobby where he met Todd.

"You're smiling. I take it you have good news?"

"Oh yeah, doc says I'm fine. I'm in great shape, tens all across the board, a clean bill of health."

Azraa'el stood among the two friends, still listening and still unseen.

"Cool man. I took off the rest of the day, so what do you wanna do." Todd asked.

"I feel like a weight has been lifted off my head, I feel like doing something crazy. Let's go climb a freaking mountain," he said smiling

"Hey, its two o'clock. Let's get something to eat," Todd suggested.

"Sounds good to me. I feel great. I feel renewed. Could this whole angel thing just be in my mind?"

"You tell me. You're the only one who's seen him," Todd replied jokingly as they left the hospital.

CHAPTER 15

SEDUCTRESS

Jonathan and Todd ended up at a local bar, celebrating his so-called new lease on life; the two friends had many drinks, and Todd, always the supplier, passed Jonathan the intoxicating smoke.

Jonathan stared at it and looked at Todd with suspicion, thinking this is the very thing that triggered the craziness he's been experiencing, but the thought quickly subsided.

"Hey man, its good stuff, stop worrying, 'it's just weed, same as before. Now let's go outside for a smoke."

Todd put his hands on Jonathan's shoulders walking behind him, and he led him out of the bar. While the two friends were outside, a beautiful young woman took a seat at the bar right next to where Jonathan had been sitting. She had golden blond hair that fell down her back, soft green eyes, beautiful fair skin, and fiery red lipstick.

She wore a tight blue dress cut just above the knees, with a revealing neckline that showed off her breasts; it hugged her body the way a man hugs a woman. After a few minutes of indulging, the men walked back inside laughing and joking, feeling even more euphoric than they did ten minutes earlier. As they approached the bar, they spotted the woman and shoved each other for position to meet her first.

"Well isn't this a surprise, I walk outside for a smoke with my friend and look what God let fall from heaven, an absolutely stunning woman," Todd proclaimed with an intoxicated tongue.

"Sorry, Todd, but God had nothing to do with it," the woman replied, both men now looking surprised.

Todd asked, "Do I know you, have we met before?"

"No, but it's nice to meet you," she said as Todd grabbed her hand and kissed it.

"And you too, Jonathan,"

A look of curiosity came over the men's faces again; they simultaneously looked at each other.

"Hey, how do you know our names? Did Stephanie send you in here? Where is she? I wanna talk to her," Jonathan asked while looking around.

"No, it was probably Emily, it was her right? She's checking up on me. See, this is why we're having problems. She doesn't trust me, I just can't be bothered," complained Todd.

"Guy's, Guy's, Guy's, I don't know who you're talking about; I'm not here to spy on you, so relax."

"Then how do you know our names?" she smiled seductively and replied, "I asked the bartender if anyone was sitting here, and he said, yeah Todd and Jonathan, so take it easy."

"Did I tell you how beautiful you are," Todd interjected. "Yes, yes, you're unbelievably gorgeous. Bartender, can we get refills and give her whatever she wants, my car, my apartment, whatever she wants, because you ...are drop-dead gorgeous."

"Why thank you, Jonathan."

"Hey, you know our names, now tell us yours."

"My name is Arianna, and I'll have scotch please."

"Arianna hmm . . . do you live around here?"

"No I don't live around here."

"So where do you live, where are you from?" Jonathan asked.

"I live all over everywhere, you know, wherever my work takes me. I'm kinda like a free agent," she said as the bartender handed her the drink.

"Yeah, what exactly is it that you do? My buddy and I are brokers, doing real well, you know," Todd said with an heir of smugness.

"Well ... I kind of run interference for my boss. I keep potential people from going over to the other team as opposed to joining us."

Todd and Jonathan giggle. "Pardon me, but what's that pay?" Todd asked.

The men laughed, as she moved closer to Todd and spoke softly. "The satisfaction of defeating the other team, knowing I planted a seed of doubt in the mind of the person about the other side, knowing I made it harder for a person to believe or accept anything about the other side, that's enough pay for me, got it Todd?" she pointed her finger in his chest as she gulp down her drink.

"My god! You smell like peaches," Todd said.

"Thank you, but I'm not for you."

"Do you have a boyfriend, are you married?" Jonathan asked.

"Dumb-question Jonathan, now that's just stupid," Todd said.

"What?"

"Never ever bring up the other guy when you're making your pitch. You'll have to excuse my friend, he's been drinking a little, well actually, he's been drinking a lot. He just lost his girlfriend; he's having a hard time at work. It's been a rough week for him, and he's pretty unstable if you really wanna know, now me on the other hand, I just might be what you're looking for."

"Well to answer your question, no, I'm not married, no boyfriend, no kids. I'm married to my work it's all I care about."

"Great, a smoking hot workaholic, just what I been looking for." Todd said sarcastically.

"Awe, is Todd disappointed? You shouldn't be, you have a girlfriend, remember Emily? Todd looked confused at the woman's statement."

"Oh yeah, but I think were on a break, I haven't gotten a call from her in over ...an hour, forget her."

"Whatever you say, Todd," she replied.

"Hey, let's drink a toast, the three of us," Jonathan said.

"OK, what are we toasting guys?"

"Well ... to beautiful women."

"Yeah! Todd agreed. They drank the toast.

Todd raised his glass. "Here, I got one, I got one ... you ready'? To mine and Arianna's kids."

"To the kids," said Jonathan.

"To the kids," she jokingly toasted.

"OK guy's, I have one ... to new friends."

"To new friends."

The trio spent the next hour and a half drinking. Jonathan and Todd drank to the point of stumbling, they prodded the woman for more conversation, but the mysterious Arianna evaded all serious questions.

She suddenly left her seat and went to the dance floor. She danced seductively as the two men watched from the bar. The more she moved, the more they became entranced. Todd was captivated by the woman.

"I gotta have her man, look at her, she's dancing for me," Todd gazed at her with loving eyes.

"In your dreams she's dancing for you, that dance is for me. She already said she's more interested in me," Jonathan said.

"No she didn't, you just made that up."

The men began to argue quietly over the woman. She danced seductively swinging her hair wildly. With their mouths open, the two men watched her every move. She pointed at them, and they point to themselves trying to clarify whom she was asking to come toward her, she pointed to Todd.

He spoke with stuttered speech, "Yes! I told you she wanted me." He made his way over to her. She held him close to her as to keep him from falling, but they danced for only a minute.

"Hold on sweetheart, I gotta take a leak. I'll be right back OK? Stay here. Don't go over there next to him. Stay here, OK?" he instructed the woman.

She continued her dance, and then called Jonathan to the dance floor, she grabbed him and pulled him close to her, and she whispered in his ear.

"It's you I really wanted to dance with." She kissed his cheek and neck softly and ran her fingers through his hair. He held her tightly, rubbed his body against hers, and began to fondle her. Todd returned only to find his beautiful dance partner with his friend. Frustrated, he walked over to the bar raised his glass and toasted Jonathan in a sarcastic way, he screamed out.

"Hey, thanks a lot, friend!"

Jonathan was totally hypnotized by the seductress; they danced erotically, as she led him by the hand off the dance floor, she walked toward the woman's bathroom. Jonathan tried to fight her off; a woman's bathroom was not where he wanted this to happen.

Todd yelled from the bar, "No! Don't go there!"

But, she kissed Jonathan, and he quickly gave up the fight.

"I want you to relax and don't worry about anything, forget about your girlfriend, forget about work."

She sat him down on the toilet and lifted her dress; they could hear the music from the other room helping to set the mood. They kissed passionately; he stroked the back of her neck with his fingers and pulled her hair gently, he tugged on the straps of her dress lowering them to reveal her full and perky breasts.

She ran her fingers through his hair and nibbled on his cheeks; kissing and biting his bottom lip, she violently pulled open his shirt, popping the buttons off as she playfully dug her perfectly manicured nails into his chest. He leaned her back and began kissing and sucking her breast, he slid his hand under her dress and massaged her inner thigh; she moaned, which excited him even more.

She leaned forward kissing him on the neck and slowly began kissing his chest. She worked her way down to his stomach and then looked up at him with a seductive grin. He looked at her with anticipation, and she unbuckled his pants grabbed hold of him and buried her face into his lap. His eyes rolled back in his head, and he closed them and enjoyed the ecstasy. As he played with her hair then held her head in place, she jumped up and sat in his lap and rocked back and forth on him, she whispered his name. He held her tightly, thrusting his body as she rocked faster; he told her she was beautiful.

In the tight quarters they occupied, there lovemaking became violent, he stood up with her; she wrapped her legs around him, they banged into the wall smashing the mirror that hung on it. He spun around and fell back against the door, partially opening it; she reached behind him and closed it back, he held her up as he thrust himself into her rapidly. He screamed her name. He turned her around so she faced the wall and he entered her from behind, he thrust hard in rapid successions. She yelled out his name. Simultaneously, they both yelled out in ecstasy and they finished where they started—an intoxicating, twenty-minute sexual encounter, sitting on the toilet in the women's bathroom. As they left their pleasure room, Jonathan walked out with his shirt and pants undone and yelled out as if he were victorious in battle.

Arianna walked over to the bar and kissed Todd on the cheek. He looked at her annoyed.

"Oh, a kiss on the cheek for me, is that my consolation prize? Wow, I get the cheek kiss while you give him the full course meal, gee thanks."

She hugged and kissed Jonathan.

"I have to run now; I had a great time with you guys."

"No, where are you going, don't leave," Jonathan begged.

"I have to go now, but don't worry about anything. I'll see you again. Just know the connection we had tonight will never be forgotten," Jonathan grabbed the woman by the hand.

"Arianna, don't leave, stay here and hang out with us. Hell, stay and hang out with me."

"I'm sorry, but it's getting late and I really should be going, don't worry we'll see each other again for sure."

She walked toward the door, but before exiting, she turned and blew a kiss to her new friends. They simultaneously waved good-bye. Todd was disappointed and Jonathan was bursting with excitement at the possibility of seeing her again. Sadly for him, that day would never come.

"OK, fill me in, how was she?"

"Why Todd, whatever do you mean?" Jonathan joked.

"Come on, you know what I mean, you go into the bathroom with her, you come out twenty minutes later like fucking King Kong. Now tell me, rub it in my face, how was she?"

"Oh no, I didn't get her phone number," Jonathan ran after her. He walked outside the bar, he looked left he looked right but no Arianna.

"Damn it," he walked back inside the bar looking dejected.

"She's gone and I didn't get her number. How am I gonna meet up with her again? I got no way to contact her."

"Forget that, how was she?"

"She was great, she was better than great. I never felt anything like that before. She was fabulous, probably the best I ever had."

"No way, better than Steph?"

"I'm gonna have to say yes, even better than Steph," he said with a smile.

"Did she do everything?"

"Why whatever do you mean Todd?" he said again joking.

"Awe, come on man, cut the bullshit. Did she do the do, did she blow you?"

"That would be a yes, my good man, and she was a-ma-zing."

"You lucky bastard, you stole her from me tonight."

"Here we go again."

"Yeah, yeah ... yes you did, as soon as I walked away, ya jumped right in my grave; well I hope you're proud of yourself."

"Hey, you know the rules, move your feet lose your seat."

"Yeah whatever, it's getting late. We better start heading home, we gotta work tomorrow. that's if you're going in?" Todd asked.

"I think I will make it to work tomorrow. Doc gave me a clean bill of health; I'm hanging with my boy; I met a beautiful new girl; and I'm feeling fine."

"Yeah ... great ... yippee for you."

"Hey, don't be that way, come on, let's have one more for the road OK, and then will go.... I'm gonna make a toast."

"What are we toasting?" Todd asked.

"I wanna toast to you ... for conceding to me."

"OK, enough bragging, you got the girl. I didn't, we know this already."

"And ... and ... a new lease on life, looking forward ... forward not back, no more crazy talk about you know who."

"Alright, now you're talking, and I'll drink to that."

"Now ... now we can go, are you ready?"

"I'm ready, yep time to go." The two friends exited the bar and waited for cabs, Jonathan going downtown, Todd going uptown. As they waited, they laughed and joke about the eventful night. Jonathan continued his antagonizing of Todd on how he won the girl. Their cabs arrived simultaneously. They shook hands and wished each other safe rides home.

CHAPTER 16
THE CONFRONTATION

At 9:15 p.m., Jonathan arrived home and stumbled through the door, singing and feeling great about the wonderful day he had, he fell down on the couch, arms stretched out and smiling from ear to ear. He laid there for a few minutes and remembered his plans to go to work tomorrow. He rolled off the couch, stood up and clumsily walked down the hall to the bathroom. He put his head in the sink and ran water over it, trying to refresh himself from the intoxicating liquor he enjoyed so much tonight.

He stood up, looked in the cracked mirror, and shook his head to get rid of the excess water running down his face. He pointed his finger at the man in the mirror and began to laugh aloud. He walked back to the kitchen, put on a pot of coffee, and timed it for five minutes, then stumbled back to the couch, laid down and shut his eyes.

Five minutes became twenty minutes, twenty minutes became an hour; Jonathan had slept an hour and a half before being awakened by a thunderous knock at the door and a beeping coffee pot. He lay there wanting to ignore both. He heard a second knock at the door and yelled out, "Go away!" A third knock had him roll off the couch. The coffee pot continued beeping, and he looked toward the kitchen but then walked to the door and opened it. There stood Azraa'el.

"Hello, Jonathan."

"What the hell are you doing here?"

"I thought you might enjoy some company, you look like you had a rough night," the angel said as he pushed past him and entered the apartment.

"For your information, I had a great night, but I guess it's all over now that the grim reaper has arrived."

The angel laughed.

"I thought I was done with you." Jonathan said.

"I just came by to see how you're doing."

"What do you care how I'm doing? It's been made clear you don't like me, and I sure as hell don't like you."

"This is not about likes or dislikes. I'm visiting you for one reason and one reason only."

"Yeah, whatever, I'll have you know I been to the doctor, got a check-up from head to toe, and he found nothing wrong with me. He 'says I'm in great shape, and I asked him if I was in danger of dying, and he said no."

"I was there Jonathan, through all your examinations. I heard the results, and I was right by your side every step of the way. Congratulations, I'm glad you're in great shape and have a clean bill of health. Dr. Bashir's is a very good doctor, but who told you, you were gonna die from some incurable disease; I know I never indicated how you would leave this realm."

"Hey, I'm not listening to you. The doctor gave me good news, and I went out and celebrated, I even found a new girl."

"You mean the girl you and Todd fell for at the bar?"

"Yeah, that's right. What did you do, follow us all night?"

"The one you took to the bathroom, a woman's bathroom, and had sexual relations, I guess that could be a nice place to spend a romantic evening with the woman of your dreams, in the bathroom of a bar. Arianna, right? Yes, she has captured many a fool with her beauty."

Jonathan looked confused. "How do you know her?"

"Jonathan, that woman you're so ready to claim is a rebel, and I don't mean rebel in the James Dean, Madonna kind of way, I mean rebel in a more spiritual way, as in rebel angel."

"What do you mean?"

"I mean, son, she's an angel, a descendant of those who I, along with my brothers and sisters, have cast out of the spiritual realm for rebelling against the Most High. I see you have allowed her to accomplish something she was unable to do with the other men that have fallen victim to her beguiling ways."

"Yeah, what's that?

"That is for me to know and you to find out."

Jonathan looked confused and started having flash backs of the sexual encounter and the woman telling him that their connection would be forever.

"So, she's an angel. I actually think it's kind of cool."

"Of course you do."

"Yeah that's right. She was nice to me and she's beautiful."

"She's not what you think she is son, she's an angel, but she is not like me."

"Like you, ha! Thank God for that."

"No Jonathan, I serve the Most High, I rank high among the spiritual beings, I exist in all realms, and I am a lord, a Supreme Being. The Most High looks upon me with great favor. I am the lord of souls." As the angel spoke these words, the clock hit twelve. "And now you have three days left on earth!"

Jonathan stared at the angel with anger and went into a drunken tirade. "FUCK YOU! I'M SICK OF YOU THREATENING ME WITH THIS BULLSHIT! I'm not gonna die. I'm not gonna let it happen. You know if you work for God, you need to go back and learn some bedside manner because you really suck at it! I think God made a big mistake sending you to do his dirty work; you're rude, crass and obnoxious, and I'll tell you something else, I think you and your precious Most High are getting your asses kicked down here by Arianna and her kind. The world is a shit hole, and I don't see any of your so-called spiritual beings down here trying to clean this crap up. Well you know what, tomorrow I'm gonna call Arianna, I'm gonna find her and I'm gonna be with her because she's what I want, SO TO HELL WITH YOU AND ANY BODY LIKE YOU! Now what do you think of that?"

The angel stared at Jonathan and pierced him with his vision, immediately causing him to vomit and rid him of the intoxicants coursing through his body. Azraa'el turned away from him and stood still with his eyes closed, as if he were in deep thought. Suddenly, the crescendoing sound of a shofar resonated throughout the apartment.

As Jonathan regained his composure, he put his hands over his ears. The sound of the blaring horn was deafening. The angel stretched his arms out to the side and slowly began to grow in stature. An immense white light, the brightest light ever seen by man, began to explode from him; the light surrounded him and became his aura.

Jonathan stood frozen in fear. The terror showed in his eyes; they were wide and locked on the angel, and, after a few seconds, he quickly crossed his arms over his face trying to shield his eyes from the light of the magnificent being. He cried out as the noise shook his body and the apartment rumbled. The floors cracked, pictures fell from the walls, and tables came off the floor. The light grew brighter and brighter, yet Jonathan was unable to move. Azraa'el mimicked the sound of the universe and began to hum in a low pitch. At this, the inside of the apartment shook more violently, and Jonathan looked around, wishing to run and hide himself, but the lord of souls, knowing his thoughts, would not allow him to retreat.

He held Jonathan in place, telling his limbs "do not carry him away." The body parts obeyed and Jonathan was forced to bear witness. Then, slowly the angel turned to face him and continued to grow, reaching the height of twenty feet, he looked down at the pitiful human and smiled.

Jonathan overcome with fear, began to plead with folded hands and tears falling down his face, to be let free from the angel's presence.

Now the entire physicality of the angel had gone from bright white to a gold color, and, for Jonathan, it was like looking into the sun. Suddenly a colorful vortex of energy shot through the skylight of the apartment, along with it appeared three small angelic beings standing a mere twelve inches in height. They came down slowly on the vortex carrying a burgundy robe, a golden crown, and a gold and ruby scepter, all fit for a Supreme Being. They circled above and around the great being. After three revolutions, they stopped midair and shouted, "PEACE BE UPON AZRAA'EL, LORD OF SOULS!"

Azraa'el lowered his head as the three beings draped over his shoulders the cloak of supremacy; they placed on his head the gold crown, and handed him the gold and ruby scepter. He then stood twenty-five feet in height.

Jonathan paralyzed with fear, unable to speak, with tears in his eyes, almost crumbled to pieces at the sight of the angels overwhelming appearance.

He looked up at Azraa'el and screamed out in agony, but his cry was drowned out by the still sounding shofar. He now knew he was in the presence of absolute power. The three beings drifted down to the right of Azraa'el; they became still and spoke with him, saying, "Lord Azraa'el and soul collector, let us take apart this man, for he is one of the wretched, he has cursed your name and shunned your power, and, even more, he speaks against our beloved Creator. Steeped in sin, he is a murderer from his early days and he is guilty of all we have witnessed. Even as his days come to an end, he is shown power by one who is in full authority to take his soul, and yet he still protests and has doubt, not only that but he has spoken lies against the Most High our Creator."

The angel heard the words of the lesser angelic beings and responded. "Far be it for me to allow any spiritual being to take the life of a mere man, for you would surely lose your prominence in the spiritual realm. You would do better to hold back your wrath; if not, then for sure a greater wrath would befall you. So, be at peace but remain present and bear witness to this event and know that I carry out the decree of our Lord and Creator."

Azraa'el focused his attention on Jonathan, he knelt down in front of him, all twenty-five feet of him, and with a deep echoing voice, he asked, "Do you still think the Most High made a mistake?" Then he blew the breath of life at Jonathan, knocking him off his feet into the wall. Jonathan lay there for a minute, and then suddenly he began to convulse violently, the apartment maintained the presence of power, and the angel stood up and took two steps back, for he knew the reason for the convulsion. His golden aura instantly changed back to white; he stood with his arms crossed and watched as the ethereal Jonathan also known as the soul, emerged. Looking misty with a transparent light-blue color, it hovered over Jonathan's lifeless body and spoke with the voice of a child.

"Peace be upon you, Azraa'el, lord of souls."

"Peace be upon you, soul, but why have you left your body without permission? You are in great error and are in danger of committing the ultimate sin."

"I know Lord but the man has transgressed all boundaries, and I am here to plead with you that you not hold me accountable for his words thoughts or actions."

"Your plea would have been heard as you travel the spiritual realm while the man sleeps, besides did you not walk with him all the days of his life, why do you petition now?"

"I am not a willing participant in the acts against his fellow man. Each time, before he would commit a sin, I urged him through his conscious to be righteous and turn away from his negative thoughts, but his mind would fight me, his spirit would fight me, and his physical being would act and overpower the soul, leaving me in distress. Now he has sworn allegiance to the rebels, and worse than that, he has cursed the Most High, Creator of all of the levels of existence. I seek forgiveness for him, for he is against all things spiritual and will not be aware until you come for him, and return us to the spiritual realm, so forgive us, Azraa'el, lord of souls."

"You are mistaken in coming to me with your complaints of the man, you know as well as I, the Most High hears and knows all the interactions between the soul and the physical being. We know your disdain for his transgressions, and you are not held accountable for them, but re-enter the body now, lest he expire before his time, for then I would surely hold you accountable." The soul stood silent as it looked over at its lifeless body with reluctance to return to it.

"I am a servant of the Most High and am at your mercy Lord Azraa'el. I pray that you will not be long in removing me from this body, may peace be upon you."

Jonathan's soul sadly reentered the body as violently as it exited, and as the body lay convulsing on the floor, the energy in the apartment began to dissipate; the sound of the shofar faded; and the light around the angel grew dim. His height diminished; the lesser angels retrieved his robe, crown, and scepter; and his demeanor and posture became subtle, and, as the presence of power left the apartment, Azraa'el became as he was before Jonathan's verbal assault.

The angel walked over to him and placed one hand on his chest and one hand on his right leg, and stopped him from shaking. Jonathan sat up quickly, his breaths were short and fast, he looked around as if he were lost. It was then 4:00 a.m.

The angel stepped back and readdressed him. "What you have witnessed was a true spiritual phenomenon. I did show you an inkling of how I appear at times in the spirit world. Three entities did come down through the vortex to take your life, and while you were in a state of confusion, your soul did escape your body and speak against you. You've made your life a disaster, you've ignored your soul and turned away from all things spiritual and engrossed yourself in the material aspects of this world, but I am not here to judge you Jonathan, I am here for your soul."

Jonathan sat with his knees pulled to his chest rocking back and forth, crying like a child.

"You are a pitiful sight right now, but I feel no compassion for you or anyone who speaks disparagingly of the Most High. Your days are limited, and it might serve you well to seek forgiveness from the one who forgives."

The angel walked over to the door, open it, and walked out. He turned and faced Jonathan, held up three of his fingers, indicating that he had three days left, and then vanished.

CHAPTER 17

SHARON THE HELPER

The angel appeared in Chicago at the home of an elderly woman caring for her cancer-stricken daughter; he emerged through the wall and remained in the ethereal form. As he watched the forty-year-old woman, he felt compassion for her ability to overcome her pain. Although weak from the debilitating disease, she refused to be bedridden.

She stood staring out her bedroom window wondering what physical complication she would have to endure today. A statuesque beauty before her condition, radiation took its toll on her, as it does most cancer patients. The hair loss and extreme decline in weight made her avoid looking in the mirror because the sight of her own image caused her to cry.

The angel sat in a chair in the corner of her bedroom, observing and listening to her thoughts, he felt sympathy, as her physical limbs, spirit, and soul spoke with him, asking to leave their body. He stood up, closed his eyes, and communicated telepathically with Rafiqiel, his second in command. "She is ready, Rafiqiel. Come forth, you requested to be part of this helpful servant's return, you requested to meet her. Now come forth," he said commandingly.

Rafiqiel appeared instantly, and the two supreme beings smiled at each other. They knew of this woman and felt privileged to meet her. As she continued to gaze out the window, the room became bright, and the withering flowers on her nightstand began to bloom again. The atmosphere was charged, and a pulsating energy lit up the room.

Oblivious to the change around her, the woman continued daydreaming until she noticed her reflection in the window, she stared at herself, she touched and caressed her face, and suddenly realized that her face was full again, no more drawn in unhealthy look. She smiled and thought it was just the windowpane adding weight to her face. Her head was wrapped in a scarf with a thick strand of hair hanging out from it, startled by this; she peered into the windowpane closer.

One hour ago, she had been completely bald. She looked harder and then raised her hand and pulled on the strand of hair and gasped in shock. She pulled off the scarf and ran her hand over her head, and felt a full head of curly, beautiful locks; her hair was just the way she wore it a year ago, before her deadly disease. "I must be dreaming," she thought, as she looked herself over; her weight had returned. She ran to the full-length mirror pinned to her bedroom door and let out a scream. She touched herself all over.

"My breasts, my butt, my legs, I'm beautiful, oh my god Ma!" This must be a joke somebody's playing a horrible joke on me." She ran to the bathroom in her bedroom to check that mirror. She giggled with disbelief and pinched herself to make sure she wasn't dreaming. She walked quickly back into her bedroom.

"I feel great, I look great, what's going on?" She walked over to the door, opened it, and screamed down to her mother, "Ma, come quick!" She continued admiring herself in the mirror for the next five minutes, overjoyed she danced around the room and thought, "This is a miracle. I prayed for my health and God heard me." She quickly got down on her knees at the side of her bed and began to pray thankfully. "Thank you, God. I don't know what happen here, but thank you, thank you, thank you," she rose to her feet and walked toward the door and yelled for her mother again, "Ma, what are you doing down there?"

She went back to the mirror and continued looking at herself, smiling. She backed away. She sat by the window and waited for her mother to come to her bedroom. "Am I dead? I must be dead, but I can't be dead there's a car driving by, you don't see cars in heaven, and you definitely wouldn't see a car driving by in hell. What's going on? One day I look like death, the next, I'm back to my old self feeling good, looking good?" She picked up the phone and called her doctor, but there was no answer she left a frantic message.

"Hello, Dr. Brown, this is Sharon Miller, please call me at home. There's something really weird going on. You have my number. Please call me as soon as you can."

As she waited for the return phone call, she thought about how great it would be to get back to doing the things she used to do before the illness befell her. She smiled at the thought. Then she began to notice what her eyes could not focus on before, the change in the atmosphere. She then stood back and marveled at the pulsating lights and colors around the window.

She heard gentle music, and she could see and feel a presence. Knowing she was now aware of the spirit-filled room, the two supreme beings manifested in the physical. As she backed away from the window, she turned slowly to her right and saw the two angels standing together in the brightest garments ever seen by human eyes.

Azraa'el wore a royal blue jalabiya and Rafiqiel a white jalabiya. Her breath escaped her. The sight of the two beings terrified her and she felt faint, but before she could collapse, they moved toward her and supported her. Rafiqiel placed her right hand in his. Azraa'el placed her left hand in his. Simultaneously, they bowed to her and spoke. "Peace and blessings, Sharon Miller."

With fear in her eyes she stared at them suspiciously and with a trembling voice asked, "Who are you?"

"I am Azraa'el, lord of souls."

"And I am Rafiqiel, a soul collector."

Confused and still terrified, she stuttered her words. "Wh, wh, what's a soul collector?"

They smiled and spoke softly, trying to ease her fears. Rafiqiel answered, "We're here to comfort you."

"Comfort me?"

"Do not be afraid Sharon. We are spiritual beings sent by the Most High, we are not here to hurt you, we are here to comfort you. In the heavens, many are rejoicing with anticipation of your return," said Azraa'el.

"What do you mean? I don't know what you're talking about. Am I going die?"

"Sharon, you may not understand this, but you are one among very few who is considered to be an exceptional spiritual being, although you are human, your humanity is well documented here and in the spiritual realm. In your life, you made everyone else first, a comfort to anyone who knows you, always there to help the less fortunate. Even those who didn't really need your help would call on you merely because they knew you would not say no to whatever request was made of you."

She nodded in agreement. We know of your spiritual acts, which you perform every day."

She nodded in agreement, but still confused and looking nervous, she asked, "But I don't go to church, I don't go to the mosque, I don't go to the synagogue, I don't do any of those things."

Rafiqiel smiled and replied, "But you do go to the hospital and read to the sick children and bring them gifts on Christmas. You deliver food to the elderly who can't make it to the super market. You do volunteer work; your monetary donations once a month helps more than you know; your love for your fellow human being is worthy of praise, and for this, your name is praised within the spiritual world, and many wait with anticipation on your arrival."

"You make it sound as if I'm perfect. I would hardly say I'm perfect, no, no, I'm not perfect at all," she said nervously.

"Maybe not, but you are as close as humanely possible." said Azraa'el.

"As some of the inhabitants of this world have decided to put little value in the spiritual aspects of this life, we take special interest in those that do; it is your nature to be more spiritual than physical Sharon."

"I guess that's why I haven't been with a man in I don't know how long," she said jokingly.

"Again, that is your decision. We know your thoughts are mainly about how you would like to get better so that you can get back to helping people, not being able to help your fellow man hurts you more than the illness itself. Many times since you became ill, you prayed to the Most High to remove this disease, and you should know that all of your prayers are heard in the spirit world. When a person prays, the righteous spirit beings pray along with you and for you, but we know the truth behind your prayers my child, and that is to get better so that you may get back to your life's work."

"I'm a secretary, I wouldn't exactly call that my life's work."

"No, of course not. We mean your real devotion, helping people."

"Well, yes, I do love helping people."

"We know, but what proves what a great spiritual nature you have, is how unaware you are of the spiritual pioneer you've become.

Rafiqiel stepped closer to her, and she backed away. "In the spirit world you are called Sharoon El Ansaar."

"Who?"

"Sharoon el Ansaar, Sharon the helper."

She smiled and giggled. "How do you know these things about me?"

"Because we are who we say we are, spiritual beings from God ... angels," Azraa'el said.

"Even as a child, we found no fault in you. At six years old, you and four of your siblings went into the neighborhood grocery store, all of you picked up something as if you were going to pay for it. You grabbed a candy bar, and when the owner turned his back, all four of you ran out without paying, your family members thought it was funny, but your soul told you it was wrong and your spirit agreed. You turned and slowly walked back to the store with your cousins yelling for you not to go, you confessed your crime to the storeowner. He yelled at you with racial slurs and snatched the candy from your hands. He cursed at you to get out of his store; you left crying and promised yourself you would never take what was not yours again."

As tears came down her face, Sharon thought back on that day with sadness at first, then looked at the angels with a smile and wondered how they were able to recall the years gone by. "That's amazing. How do you know that? Yes, I remember that day, but how?"

"Because we are who we say we are," Azraa'el replied.

"OK, so what is all this supposed to mean?" she asked.

Rafiqiel answered her, "Your time is near, my child; there's nothing that can be done or needs to be done for you here, and we've come to return you to the Most High."

"So, I'm gonna die, is that what you're saying?"

"You will feel no pain from this day until your last; it will be as if you have no illness, and this is a mercy from the Most High."

"But, what about Ma?" She asked with tears and becoming frantic.

"I don't want her to be alone. She needs me. I'm afraid for her. there's no one else to help her. I don't want to die!" she screamed. The two beings looked at her with sadness and felt her anguish.

Azraa'el comforted her and said, "Don't be afraid Sharon, for yourself, or your mother; she will not be alone, a companion will come, a man of similar age with similar likes and dislikes. For when you are gone it will pain her, but be assured she will not hurt very long, she will remember the great daughter she gave birth to. She and her new companion will sit and talk about you for many hours and many days; she will not be alone my child. Sharon thought for a few seconds then shook her head in disagreement, and with short breaths and tears, she asked with a trembling voice,

"Well, if I'm so honored in heaven, then why do I have to die?"

"Have no doubt, my child, your soul asked to return the moment it knew of your disease. Your spirit fought to get healthy, but as time went by, your spirit became weak, and it joined the soul in wanting to return. The physical, always the follower, began to feel weak and it joined the other two. These three are ready and willing to return. The mind is the only thing not willing to let go. Your mind has been alert and functional, but the mind is imagining what is not possible, it will soon be like the rest of you, very weak. The light inside you is dimming. All the components of you are ready. Mentally, you don't want to go, but soon your mind will lose this internal battle, and, in a couple of days, you will suffer loss of consciousness, and this will happen three to four times over the next few days, and this is your mind telling you it will no longer fight the soul, spirit, or physical; the mind is ready. At that point, the Most High will not prolong life. When the Most High makes a decision it will come to pass."

She stared at the two angels. They were silent. She turned and walked over to the mirror and looked herself over; she wiped away her tears and smiled at her healthy body, she turned, faced them, and asked, "So when, when will it happen?"

And, as tears came down her face again, Rafiqi embraced her and comforted her, and when he did this, he allowed her to see herself in the spirit realm. Her spirit instantly became renewed and she felt no more concern or worry and he answered her.

"I will be escorting you back to the realm of those who need no correction of their souls, in five days."

Azraa'el approached her, bid her peace and blessings, and took leave of them. For the rest of that day, Rafiqiel entertained Sharon, performing miracles, telling her about the spirit world, and making her laugh. She had no pain and had no more concerns about her mother. On tuesday April 2000, at 2:00 p.m., Sharon died peacefully in her sleep.

CHAPTER 18
QUESTIONS AND ANSWERS

Jonathan fell asleep on the floor and woke early the next morning, confused but well aware of what took place in the apartment, he sat in the same spot for an hour reviewing the terrifying yet awe-inspiring angel's demonstration. He felt weak, barely able to stand, but he made his way to the bathroom, after urinating he moved to the sink and washed his hands, he looked in the mirror and gasped; he didn't recognize himself.

He appears to have aged ten years over night, with bags and lines under his eyes, pale skin and a head full of gray hairs, punishment for his drunken tirade against the angel. He frantically threw water over his face and hair, he walked back to the living room, moving slowly, and his body ached from the soul jumping in and out of it. He sat down on the couch and wondered what could happen next. "Holy shit, I'm gonna die," he said to himself, a shocked look on his face. He sat for a couple of minutes reliving the night's event in his mind. He grabbed the phone, his hand shook uncontrollably as he pressed the buttons and called his sister.

"Hi Jen, it's me."

"Ewe, you sound horrible. What's the matter with your voice?" she asked.

"I just had a rough night, that's all."

"You should drink some tea and honey," she said.

"Yeah, I'll try it later, but listen, would you happen to have a Bible?"

"A Bible, what do you want a Bible for?"

"I think maybe it's time I get to know—you know—GOD."

"Wow! Go figure, never saw you as the God-fearing type, but yeah, I have one, you know you can go to any church and get one."

"Nah, I'm not up for going out. Could you bring it by here? And I need it soon as possible," he said nervously.

"You're not gonna learn about God just by reading the Bible. Are you still worried about dying? That's crazy talk Jonathan."

"No, that's not it at all. I'm just anxious to get started. If you can do me this favor, I'd appreciate it."

"OK, I'll come by after work, do you need anything else?"

"No, just the book. Hey, you don't mind leaving it in the mailbox, I mean I might be sleep or something, ya know?"

"Oh, OK, whatever you want."

"Thanks sis, good-bye." Jonathan anxiously paced in the apartment most of the day regretting his every bad decision and act in his life; his telephone rang nonstop, but he ignored it. He looked around the apartment and had flash backs of what happen the night before. He remembered the angel growing in stature. He looked up at the skylight and wondered how the three beings came through it without breaking the glass. He shook with fear at the thought of them wanting to destroy him, and, although he felt the effects of his soul leaving his body, he had no recollection of it.

"Aw man. I'm gonna die, what the fuck! What's that like? I can't imagine me not being here, "Jonathan Krause dead at 28" damn! But how, I'm not sick, is somebody gonna kill me, a car accident?"

He thought for hours, imagining how his death would happen. One thing for sure, he had no more doubt that it would. At 6:30 p.m., the doorbell rang. He ran to the window and looked down to the street to see whom it was, his sister dropping off the Bible. He peeked through the blinds so she wouldn't see him, after a few minutes, he went down wearing pajamas and a bathrobe, got the book out of the mailbox, and then ran back upstairs.

He sat down on the couch and immediately started reading; the last time Jonathan picked up a Bible, he was as a ten-year- old kid attending church with his parents. Jonathan sat and read for most of the night, he drank wine, and laughed at some of the things he read, but then he became angry and started skimming through the book, hoping to find the angel's name—he slammed it closed, got up, and started pacing the floor again.

"Where are you? Are you kidding me with the shit that's going on in this book?" He raised the book to the ceiling. "Where are you Azraa'el?" At the sound of his name, the angel appeared instantly, startling Jonathan, who jumped backed away, and raised his hands in a defensive manner.

"I didn't mean to yell. I'm sorry."

"How are you, my son," The angel noticed the Bible on the coffee table.

"I see you been reading."

"Yeah, I just thought I could try to understand—God," he said sarcastically.

"So far all I see in this book is sex, murder, back stabbing, and deceit—the only thing missing is the drugs and rock-n-roll. No disrespect, but what the hell was God doing while all this crap is going on? I just wanna understand."

"When I suggested you seek forgiveness from the one who forgives, I thought you might think quietly to yourself about your very existence, how you could've been a better person. How you might ask forgiveness about the bad decisions you've made in this life. I hoped you would feel remorse for ever being born; confess even to yourself your crimes against your fellow man. When man feels regret, we listen. The Most High hears those who have regret, to feel regret about a thing can be a humbling of the spirit, and to be humble is always good. I don't see that in you as of yet Jonathan. What I see is an inquiring mind, wanting to know why or how, which is not a bad thing. We insist that man learn all there is to know about the workings of the Most High, but yours is an inquisition for the sole purpose of trying to prevent the inevitable, when you're asking why, what you really mean is why me? It's a little late to be trying to find the Most

High in any book. I wish I could applaud your efforts, but I can't, because this is just another selfish act on your part."

"Ok, you might be right about that, but it still doesn't answer why, even these men of this so-called God were doing crazy shit back then?"

"Those people, and the way they lived, are from a different time in human history. I don't see the point in talking to you about that. Just know every one of them met with me or my legion, and no one will escape this realm except they meet the soul collectors."

Jonathan sat quietly for a minute shaking his head annoyed by the angel. "Alright there were a couple of times in my life where I thought I should have died and I always thought that it must have been some kind of divine intervention. I remember being about nineteen or twenty years old. I drove a 1982 Nissan Pulsar. Me and a friend of mine were hanging out driving around drinking beers. We did this for a couple hours before going to pick up my girlfriend at the time; she worked at this mall a few miles from where we lived. It was about 10:30 at night when we start out to go get her. We get on this service road—it's like a small three lane highway—and we're doing about thirty miles an hour. I see this car in the middle lane, and I'm coming up on him fast because I thought he was moving: his lights are on; it looked like he was moving; but he wasn't. He was broke down right there, but here we come, too fast to stop and, at the very last second, I turned the wheel and just missed crashing into the guy. My life flashed before my eyes. I just knew we were dead; it was like someone else took control of the steering wheel right at the last second."

"Yes, we reviewed your near death experience; it was only near death because you were drinking, but any way, the near death experiences, many people experience this, and just as you think you're going to die, at that moment you confess the Most High.

"I didn't do that."

"You did do it, after you survived and after you used your foul language, you did say "Oh God," and we accept that as acknowledgment of the Most High. You could have a near death experience everyday of your life, but if it's not your time, you will not die."

"Yeah, well, what about people that commit suicide, we know it's not their time, it's them taking things into their own hands?" Jonathan replied.

"Oh, but it is their time; we know this is how they've chosen to return to the Most High. Those who choose suicide have thought about it many times before they actually go through with it. Their mind urged them to do it, and at this time, the spirit becomes weak and defeated; the physical body doesn't want to do it because it has to do the actual deed, and it can be painful, but it goes along with the spirit. The soul becomes irritated, happy, angry, and sad all at once, because it's always ready to reconnect with the Most High, but never as a suicide, and this is the cause of the person's erratic behavior, and why his fellow man labels him crazy beforehand."

Jonathan nodded his head as if he understood the angel's explanation. "People have said to me that if you kill yourself you can't go to heaven. Is this true?"

"Wrong, Jonathan. The suicides are ushered into the spirit world immediately and without question. The spiritual realm is a comfort to all of the Most High's creation. Those who commit suicide felt defeated in this realm and lost their will to live; they're mind made them believe there was no other way, and that they shouldn't go on. Their mind is wrong, so once they die, the seraphim [obedient angels] grab hold of them and immediately go to work repairing every aspect of their being, mind, body, soul, and spirit. Trust in this, Jonathan. You will all go to heaven, but how you exist there, will be your choice."

"How will it happen, how will I die, what time will it happen?" Jonathan became teary eyed as he spoke of the inconceivable event.

"Ever since you came into my life, all I've done is fall apart. I die a little bit every day–you're right, I don't think it's fair. It's like your torturing me; you're not physically hurting me, but I'm going crazy. I just wanna know why, why I have to die, I'm too young? I have a lot of life to live. There are far worse people out there than me, and I feel like I'm being picked on," he said, shaking his head in frustration. "It's just stupid."

"Since the beginning, every creature, large and small, from human to ant, has asked me this question, why? The answer is the same as always, it's your time to go. You've lived your life positively or negatively, and you say you have a lot of life left to live, but we say no, you have lived a full life, whether you are an infant that dies immediately after birth or you live to be one hundred. Although I was created with the knowledge of time of death for every living entity and am the appointed soul collector, only the Most High can say why. All of your questions about this life will be answered by the one who possesses all the knowledge of every age and time of human history and beyond. This is not about picking on you: it's about it being a person's time, it's about me taking hold of what rightfully belongs to the Most High and returning it."

"I still think it sucks. So, what, is God angry with me for the things I've done? I'll change—tell him I'll change."

"If the Most High were to get angry with you, you would immediately cease to exist. The Lord absolutely does not get angry, for if the Creator were to get angry, it would imply that something or someone has frustrated the Supreme Being, and nothing could be further from the truth. The Most High is all you can imagine a person place or thing to be, magnified one million times—the Supreme Being is above the human error you fall victim to.

The Most High looks upon all creation as merely a child, whether you are animate or inanimate you are just a child on the grand scale of things. All creation should accept this and have a childlike fear of the Creator, yet you should gravitate toward the Supreme Being, for that is your final destination in the end. The Most High is not angry with you, there is a hope that you will elevate to a more spiritual being while still in this realm—we know your difficulties, we knew there would be struggles between men, one to another; there was war in the spirit world, why would we think you wouldn't have them here. Many have come in the name of God to inspire men to live as brothers, but many more have come to destroy that idea. So, we watch with great expectation that the human family will remember that they are all connected and that no group is better than the other. If the Most High had a favorite person or group, then you would have reason not to show reverence to your Creator; the Most High does not play favorites to any group or any one person. We only have hope that you will elevate and choose spirituality as your way. If you maintain this way of living while on your journey, we are happy for you, and when you pray, we also pray that the spiritual gifts descend and come through you."

"Well what about hell? I know I don't want to end up there?"

"Hell is for those who deliberately injure their soul by constantly committing crimes against nature, other human beings, or any being for that matter. They've taken an oath to themselves and declared war on all things spiritual, and what is agreed upon to be right. When their physical life is over, they will be captured by four of my soul collectors and made to watch what you might call a movie; this movie will be about them and every action and thought they had. After watching their movie, they will be asked, "Will you work to elevate and repair the soul the Merciful One has blessed you with? We hope the person will agree and remain a part of the Most High as an everlasting soul. But, we know they will have no such desire to elevate, even after reaching the spiritual realm, and that soul will remain stagnate, and it will be in a state of frustration and repetition. It will not vibrate, and the Most High will not allow it to gravitate toward the highest level until the spirit of that person has burned out. When the spirit burns out, the soul will burn out and become true essence, which is the mist and particles of the Supreme Being. The true essence or mist will then meld back into the Most High for reconnection and transformation—make no mistake, it does not harm the Creator if you decide not to exist anymore. The Most High always was and will always be; nothing and no one can change that."

Jonathan contemplated the angel's words for a few seconds, and then asked, "So when do I get to meet this God? Will he want to meet me?"

"You must first get rid of the slight doubt about there actually being a Supreme Being, and, after your physical death, there should be an immediate transformation of the soul and spirit, and a feeling of relief, of being back where you belong, and of course a feeling of joy should be felt when you reach the heavens. Those who leave this world and arrive in the afterlife confused about what has transpired and unwilling to accept their death will have to work on their spirituality before basking in the presence of the glorious one. A warning to you, Jonathan: don't have the soul collectors play your movie, for many who refused to be humble, it is an embarrassing thing, better to be humble now then be forced to be humble later. So, when the question comes to you Will you elevate? let your answer be Yes, I will elevate. They stood silently as Jonathan once again contemplated his death.

"Will you tell me?"

"Tell you what?" the angel replied.

"How will it happen; it's been on my mind for a week. I'm begging you, please tell me, how's it gonna happen?"

"I will not tell you how. If I did, I would contribute to you trying to disrupt the natural order of things, and you would take steps to try to prevent the inevitable," Jonathan looked at the angel angrily and responded. "No, I don't think so. According to you, I've only got one day left!"

"Regardless, this is a law established from the beginning by the Most High and put upon me to uphold for as long as I am the soul collector, and I will up hold my obligation to the life giver."

"If you have any kindness in you, if you have an ounce of mercy in you, you'll grant me this one thing–just please tell me."

"I am merciful and kind, but my allegiance is to one whose authority cannot be challenged. You are not the first to ask these silly questions, nor the last, and your attempts to provoke me are futile. I've heard this all before. When a person exits the womb, they come into the world crying and screaming, realizing they are no longer a child of paradise and now wishes to be back in the spirit world. As times goes by, they adapt to this world, and thoughts of the spiritual world begin to fade. After even more time goes by, they remember either that they are a spiritual being or they totally forget their true nature. Many come to love this material realm so much that when their short journey here is complete, they are reluctant to leave."

Jonathan sat down on the couch and buried his face in his hands; tears came to his eyes, as the angel stood a few feet away from him, completely unmoved by his emotional pleas.

"Well, what's it like there? How's it gonna be for me? Can you at least give me that?" He said in a barely audible voice.

Azraa'el walked around the apartment investigating every inch of it and then replied, "For a person who never thought about how his actions affected this world, not to mention the spiritual world, you sure are interested now, aren't you? In heaven, whatever you wish or think will be granted to you, as long as you are in accordance with the same natural order there, as here. If you wish to exist in an atmosphere where the weather is always beautiful, where the sun shines all day, with blue skies and plush green pastures, where flowers bloom at your request, where rainbows appear like clockwork, in honor and gratitude to the Most High for creating such a magnificent place, where peace has no opposition, it will be granted to you.

You will be able to communicate with the four-legged creatures; they will communicate back; and no fear would exist between you. The birds of heaven would sit on your shoulder and sing to you the songs of praise they've created for the Most High, in hopes that you would sing along with them.

If you wish to exist in a realm that would give you the four seasons, such as you have here on your planet, it will be granted: waterfalls, rivers, and lakes for you to swim in, or any sport that you are used to doing here, will be granted, mountains to reside on, other beings to meet, relatives and friends who have been long gone from the physical world can be reacquainted. If you, Jonathan, will seek to elevate your being, you will be given a master teacher and he or she will tutor you in the ways of spirituality, such as how to attain higher realms in the spirit world, space travel, levitation, and flight. The reading of books that reveal the truth about all the nations of the world, reading the book on whatever individual you wish to know about, past, present, and future. Yes, my son, you will be afforded any and every possibility in the spirit world, as long as you agree to work to perfect your soul. You will cry tears of joy the moment you enter paradise: the beautiful fragrance that exist on all the spiritual levels, the scenery is magnificent

my description can barely do justice to the actual place. I travel upward every five of your days, but, before entering paradise, I am scanned in the ultraviolet laser, as to leave any of your planet's poisons where they belong. The sad thing, Jonathan, is that humans have been asked to elevate while they are still in the physical realm, so that they may attain these spiritual gifts while they are still alive in this world. But, for some reason, many of you think that when your physical life ends here, you will automatically become a super being and so you have no interest in working for spirituality in this realm.

There is no question you will be a different being in as much that when you die this death, you will immediately see the truth of things. To reach the highest levels of spirituality, you must agree to an elevation, and this elevation of the spirit requires you to accept your physical death and to follow the instructions of your master teacher. In heaven, there is no disguising your true feelings, so if you say with your mouth, "I will elevate," and your spirit is saying, "No I do not wish to elevate," it will be known. Should you not wish to rise as a spirit, your teacher will take leave from you and abandon you in whatever realm you exist in, until you truly wish to elevate or you burn out of existence.

The spiritual world is pretty much like your physical world, take away the lies, racism, deception, murder, and war; this place would be as the spiritual world is, but it is clear you humans enjoy destroying each other. So, my advice to you is to elevate ...I'm going to leave you now, I don't have to tell you, but I will any way, twenty-four hours, Jonathan, just twenty-four hours." The angel walked over to the door and walked out as Jonathan stared angrily; he despised when the angel would warn him of his time left. He watched him leave, then looked over at the clock on the wall, 11:59, and stormed off to his bedroom. He lay on the bed pondering aloud his dislike for the angel, and his impending death.

"How could God have someone like him as an angel, I THOUGHT ANGELS WERE SUPPOSED TO BE GOOD!" He shouted at the ceiling slamming his fist on the bed, "WHAT'S THE POINT IN EVEN BEING BORN IF THIS IS WHAT IT ALL COMES TO? I'M TWENTY-EIGHT YEARS OLD, I'M

STILL A KID IN MOST PEOPLES EYE'S! OH, BUT AT LEAST I MADE IT TO ADULTHOOD RIGHT? NOT LIKE MIKEY AND JIMMY, THEY WERE TWELVE YEARS OLD: WHAT THE HELL'S UP WITH THAT? BUT, I GUESS THIS IS WHAT LIFE IS ABOUT, YOU'RE BORN, YOU LIVE A LITTLE, THEN YOU DIE, I GUESS I SHOULD BE GRATEFUL FOR THE TIME I HAD HERE. WELL, I'M NOT, WHY THE HELL SHOULD I BE. LIFE SUCKS, THIS WORLD SUCKS, AND THERE'S NOTHING TO BE GRATEFUL ABOUT! MY LIFE WAS FINE UNTIL THIS ASSHOLE SHOWED UP., WHY DOES HE HAVE TO FUCK WITH ME? IF I'M GONNA DIE, JUST LET ME DIE."

He paused for a few seconds and began yelling again. "WHY DOES HE HAVE TO COME AND TELL ME I'M GONNA DIE! YOU THINK THIS ISN'T FUCKING WITH THE NATURAL ORDER OF THINGS, THIS ISN'T NORMAL, AND THIS ISN'T NATURAL AT ALL. SOME SPOOK ANGEL FUCKING WITH PEOPLE!"

Jonathan paced the floor wringing his hands, nervous and scared, but then he calmed down and he thought to himself. He sat back down on the bed and looked around the apartment. "What am I gonna do with all this stuff?" He went to the kitchen, grabbed garbage bags, and started dumping his belongings into them, he came across pictures of himself and Jenny, his mother, and his father and he started to cry, slamming his fist against his chest. The thought of never seeing them again was painful. He wiped his tears and yelled out again, "IT'S NOT FAIR; IT'S NOT FAIR. I WANT YOU TO KNOW IT'S NOT FAIR. I DON'T KNOW WHAT YOU WANT ME TO DO. WHAT AM I SUPPOSED TO DO NOW?" He put his hands to his face and stood in silence. He looked over at the clock; it was 1:00 a.m. Jonathan walked into the bathroom, open the medicine cabinet, and grabbed a bottle of sleeping pills. He went to the kitchen, put two pills in his mouth, and drank half a bottle of wine. Then he went back to his bedroom and lay down. Thirty minutes later, Jonathan was in a deep sleep, but after three hours, he began to toss and turn, at times crying out "No!" Thoughts of his death entered his dreams; his bed covering became wet from his perspiration, and he moaned and asked in a muttered, low voice "Why?" His nightmares went on throughout the night.

CHAPTER 19

NEVER THOUGHT IT WOULD BE YOU

Jonathan woke the next day to blue skies and the sun brightening his bedroom, any other time, He'd welcome this beautiful day, but instead, he lay their wallowing in his approaching fate. At 10:00am, he finally dragged himself out of bed and began doing his normal routine, a shower, breakfast, and a cup of coffee. He sat down on the couch trying to enjoy it, but all he could think about was the angel.

He grabbed the television remote trying to block out the voices in his head, he went through the channels for a minute and came across a music video, it reminded him of he and Stephanie, he watched as it brought a smile to his face. He continued to tap the buttons on the remote and got annoyed when he heard the weatherman report, "75 degrees in New York City, blue skies and sunshine: it's gonna be a beautiful day." He turned it off after a minute, looked up at the ceiling as if talking to God and shouted.

"OK, I GUESS I'LL JUST SIT HERE AND WAIT TO DIE!" Jonathan sat in silence for an hour, until the phone rang. He stared at it wondering if he should even bother to answer it, and, after the fourth ring, the answering machine came on. "Hey it's me. Pick up the damn phone. I've been calling for two days. What the hell's going on?"

"Hey, Todd."

"Jonathan, where the hell ya been? I've been trying to reach you."

"I been here ..." He rubbed his hands in his eyes. "I don't even wanna tell you what went on here a couple of nights ago."

"Awe, here we go again. Are you still on that I'm gonna die shit?"

"Yeah. He came back, and if I didn't believe before, trusts me I'm a believer now, and today is the day I'm supposed to die." He began crying hysterically, "I can't believe I can even let that come out of my mouth."

"Come on, man, You're gonna be OK. Listen, Jeanine is having this pool party at her father's hotel; I'm coming over there to get you, and we're going to that party."

"No! I'm not going-I'm not going anywhere, I'm not leaving this apartment, no way. I leave here and something bad is gonna happen, I know it; so you can just count me out."

"I'm not gonna let anything happen to you, you'll be among friends, so stop worrying and trust me."

"What makes you think you can prevent anything from happening to me? You don't know what can happen once I walk out that door; freaking angel won't even tell me how it's gonna go down. I don't think so, I think I'll do better staying right here."

"Well I'm going there anyway. If you don't come out, what am I supposed to tell people, 'oh, Jonathan can't come out because an angel came and told him he's gonna die'? Come on, man."

"Hey, I don't care what you tell them, you can tell 'em whatever you want, makes no difference to me because I'm not going, I'm staying put."

"I'll see you in a little while Jonathan, because you're going to this party with me."

"Yeah, I should be a lot of fun at a party on the day I'm gonna die, yeah I can see that happening."

"Good-bye Jonathan, have your ass ready when I get there."

"Yeah, whatever." Jonathan stood up. He walked over to the window and watched the world move about, airplanes gracing the skies, down below taxicabs rushing busily through the city, people strolling hand in hand without a care in the world.

"All those people out there ... and I'm the guy he picks to kill."

Thirty minutes later, the doorbell rang, and Todd called up from the streets. "It's me, let me up," Jonathan hit the buzzer and let him up.

"What's up, buddy? Holy fuck, you look like shit. What the fuck happened to you? You're all gray, eww, what the hell.

"What's in the bag?"

"Brew, you want one?"

"Yeah."

"You really look like shit," Todd looked confused as he took in Jonathan's appearance, not understanding how he could age so much over the past two days.

"I told you the angel came back and scared the life out of me; you thought what happen to you was crazy, you won't believe what happen here Thursday night. Three other angels came through that skylight and wanted to kill me, all because I pissed them off, and he stood in this apartment, twenty-feet-tall—do you hear me? He was twenty-feet tall. He was so huge, he took up the entire space in this apartment, he started changing colors and shapes; it was amazing, but scary as hell—no man, that's it, I'm a dead man, I'm gonna die for sure."

Todd with a disbelieving smirk on his face looked at Jonathan and gulped down the beer he had in his hands. "Uh, yeah ...OK, the angel came to get you, whatever man; I'm not getting into that with you, I just came to hangout."

Jonathan finished his first can of beer in about two minutes and then opened another. "I don't know what I'm gonna do, hell what can I do?"

"Were not gonna do anything, were just gonna chill, drink and forget all this bullshit," Todd said.

"I haven't been able to think about anything except this."

"Let's talk about something else Jonathan. Hey, by the way, you got fired, the reports were fine, but Bill got fed up with your personal problems and told me to tell you not to come back, and they gave your office to loser Paul."

"What! When did this happen?"

"Tuesday."

"What, just like that, they don't even call me in to tell me to my face? Thanks a lot Todd, you could've called me!"

"We tried," he said with laughter, but you weren't answering your phone."

"Yeah well, tell Bill I said kiss my ass, ungrateful bastard. It doesn't matter any way. Hey give me another beer."

"Yep, you screwed yourself right out of a job, but at least you'll get severance pay, that should hold you for a while. Hey you know the secretary from the thirtieth floor, dark curly hair, nice body, always goes to lunch with Sarah from our legal department?"

"Yeah, what about her?"

"Well, seems you may have blown your chance with her," He said with a smile.

"How's that?"

"Sarah told me, the girl thought you were cute, but now that you don't work their anymore looks like that ship has sailed."

"Oh that's just perfect, I lose my job and a chance at the best piece of ass in the building, and I'm gonna die all in the same week—doesn't get any better than this does it?"

"No, it doesn't, cheers, buddy ... hey, look what I got," Todd pulled out a small bag.

"Awe, why'd you bring that?"

"Hey, it's your going away party right? We're just two guy's hanging out. Look in that bag, see if that blunt is in there."

"Yeah, it's right here."

"So, have you heard from Stephanie?" he asked as he broke open the cigar and poured the drugs into it.

"No, but I think about her a lot now; I should've been a better boyfriend, you know. I acted like a real jerk this past year, I took her for granted, I lied to her, played these stupid little head games, yeah I fucked that up. I wish I could see her, maybe she'll let me apologize for all that shit you know."

"Why don't you call her?"

"I tried, she wouldn't take my call. It looks like that's it for me and her, we're done."

"Well, here's a little something to ease your pain my man," he said as he passed him the intoxicant.

"I hope it's not that horse shit you gave me last week."

"Hey, my stuff is quality, don't start that again."

"Yeah, whatever."

"Hey, you got any chips in this place?"

"Yeah, I'll get them," as Jonathan walked to the kitchen Todd's cell phone rang.

"Uh, oh that's Stacy calling me from the hotel," he answered it.

"Hello ...yeah, I'm trying to get him to come out ...well right now, we're just chillin', getting our heads right, drinking, and smoking some bud. We'll get there soon as we can. Who? Sarah is there, Sarah Bennett from my office..., How'd that happen? Did she bring her friend Denise? Cool..., be there in an hour. I'm gonna get this guy to come out, even if I have to slip him a mickey and drag him there myself. Alright, see you soon. Todd hung up the phone and gave Jonathan a devious look. "Check this out Jonathan, Sarah is at the party."

"Sarah from work?"

"Yeah."

"What's she doing there?"

"She and Jeanine are cousins."

"Really?"

"Yeah, but get this, she's got her friend Denise with her too."

"And Denise would be?"

"You ready for this, dark curly hair, nice body, that's who she is."

"Ooh!"

"We gotta go to the party, man. Here's your chance."

"No, I'm not going out, I can't."

"Are you crazy, you gonna pass up this chance? Stacy says there's like twenty hot women there, we gotta go!"

"Not me, now give me another beer, and you said you were gonna hang out with me today so you gotta stay."

Todd, disappointed, flopped down on the couch.

"Your right, OK, Jonathan if this is what you wanna do, this is what were gonna do, we'll just sit here while there's a crazy party going on just thirty minutes away, with women, food, and booze. Denise, Jonathan, curly hair, nice body, she's there waiting for you, Stacy told me Brian's already asked her to get him her phone number and he's moving in for the kill, Did I mention women and booze?"

"We got weed and booze, we can party right here."

"Oh yeah, where are the women, the food? Hey you know what whatever, dude I'm here for you ... but I'd rather be there." Jonathan and Todd sat around the apartment and continued drinking and smoking for two hours.

At 5:00 p.m., Todd walks into the party dragging Jonathan along; he was too intoxicated to make it on his own, he had passed out while at home indulging.

Stacy excited to see the guys finally made it "Hey guys, I thought you two would never get here."

"Hi Stacy, I had to wait for him to fall asleep, do me a favor go out and pay the cab driver. Hey Jonathan, wake up buddy," Todd tapped his face.

"Come on man, wake up, were here".

Jonathan had been asleep for two hours and started coming out of it. Todd gave him another smack on the cheek.

"Hey, let's go. We're going inside," Jonathan, barely coherent responds.

"What ... what are we doing here, Todd? I told you I didn't wanna come out."

"Yeah, I know, but it'll be fun. Now come on, you gotta get a hold of yourself."

He struggled to get Jonathan into the hotel, a luxury building on the upper eastside of Manhattan, and as they walked through the lobby, they got approached by building security.

"Who you guys here to see?"

"I'm not here to see anybody because I don't want to be here." Jonathan griped.

"Don't mind him sir, we're here to see Jeanine Stratford."

"Well I know Miss Stratford is having quest in the pool area, but I'm still gonna have to check to see if you guys belong here. What are your names?"

"Todd and Jonathan," Todd replied. Stacy reentered the hotel from paying their cab fare.

"Hey Fred, those guys are with me. Todd you owe me twenty-five dollars."

"I wanna go home," Jonathan said.

"No way man, were here and so are the girls; you'll be fine, just relax."

"What's wrong with him?" Stacy asked.

"He's still a little buzzed from earlier. You know, we were hanging out at his place getting high."

"Well you know you guys have to be cool, Jeanine doesn't want it to get too rowdy."

"We'll be cool, right, Jonathan?"

"Whatever man, I'm not into it anyway."

They walked into the pool area; it was an Olympic-size pool, five-feet deep on one end, and twelve-feet deep on the other end. Todd waved and smiled at the mostly female guests while holding on to Jonathan. Jonathan was also energized by the small crowd, and he quickly perked up.

"Hey Jonathan, Brian's been putting the moves on the girl from your office since he got here; I heard she likes you, but if you want to go home," Stacy said slyly, trying to get him to stay.

"She's not from our office, she's on another floor, and I do wanna go home, but I guess we can stay for a little while."

"Alright, that's my boy!" Todd said excitedly.

"Hey guys, the drinks and food are over there," Stacy said as she pointed to the other side of the pool.

"Cool, I'll be right back," Todd sat Jonathan down in the chair.

"Hey, where you going? Don't leave me here alone Todd, you gotta watch out for me."

"I know, just sit here for a little bit or just stand right here. I'm gonna go get a drink. You want something, you wanna eat?"

"No, just go and come back," Jonathan demanded. As he sat there, he looked around and found it hard to take how everyone could be enjoying themselves on the day he is supposed to die. He got up and stood at the edge of the pool shaking his head in disgust as people splashed around in the water; despite the friendly atmosphere, he looked nervous and sweaty.

"Hey Jonathan, come on in!"

"What's up, Matthew? I can't, I don't have trunks," slurring his words.

"Go ask Jeanine. She's got a storage room full of 'em."

"Yeah, maybe later. Now where the hell is Todd? My head is spinning; I need to sit down," he said under his breath.

"Yo, look who I found," Todd said as he returned with a drink in hand and a young lady.

"There you are Todd, what the hell man," Jonathan said.

"Sarah, you know Jonathan?"

"Hello Jonathan."

"Hey, how ya doing Sarah?"

"Sorry about you losing your job."

"Ugh, I'll be fine; it's no biggie."

"Are you sure, I know some people I can call and…"

"No I'm fine things are happening for me as we speak, besides I got some money saved and my severance pay, that should hold me for a bit, at least until I'm back to work. I'll be fine. Don't worry about me."

"OK, I wish you the best."

"Thanks." He looked at her shaking his head as she turned away from him, knowing she has no idea what had been going on with him. "Hey uh, Sarah, your friend Denise is here right? Why don't you introduce her to John?" Todd suggested.

"Uh, Todd can I have a word with you, excuse us for a sec, Sarah," he pulled Todd to the side.

"Ay man, I'm feeling a little queasy; I think I need to lie down."

"She's about to bring the girl from the thirtieth floor over Jonathan … would you relax, or perk up, do something man."

"I know, but I don't think it's a good idea right now."

"Are you crazy? –Sarah, go get the girl for my friend," Todd urged.

"No, Sarah, don't get anybody."

"Yeah, Sarah, go get her, and we're gonna be right here. Don't listen to him. He's just nervous–bring her over. Hey what do ya think of my swimming trunks? I'm going in."

"Good for you, Todd."

"What, you're not going in?"

"No. I really want to get the hell out of here."

"Awe come on, nothings gonna happen to you, you're safe here. We know all these people plus, I'm looking out for you, I got your back from the big bad angel," Todd said sarcastically.

"Hey don't talk like that, you're gonna piss him off again."

"Yeah, I'm real scared; Look, here comes Sarah with her hot friend."

"Guys, this is Denise; Denise, this is Todd and that's Jonathan," Jonathan sprang out of his chair and tried to make himself presentable.

"You lost your job, huh?" Denise asked.

"Yeah, but I'll be alright."

"It's nice to meet you," she replied.

"Likewise."

Todd walked up behind Jonathan and whispered, "You still wanna leave; man she's beautiful, and she's almost spilling out of that bathing suit."

"So, Denise, you live around here?" Jonathan asked.

"No, I live in Brooklyn with my parents."

"Hmmm."

"I know what you're thinking," she said. "A twenty-six-year-old woman still living at home with Mommy and Daddy, but I grew up in that house, and my parents don't mind. Actually, they prefer I stay there, you know, I'm their little girl."

"No, I don't have a problem with that. I understand totally."

"So what, you're not gonna swim. I see you're fully dressed. Todd looks ready how about you?"

"I'm not up for swimming. I'm just gonna hang out and watch everybody else that's all."

"OK, whatever you say."

She walked to the edge of the pool and dipped her toes in the water. Todd walked over to her.

"Hey Denise, I'll go in if you go in with me." He grabbed her hand; she smiled and accepted his invitation, and they walked away from the pool and got a running start. They counted to three and ran hand in hand into the water. Todd put his arms around her and smiled at Jonathan, implying he was about to steal this one away from him. As the partygoers splashed around in the water, Jonathan waved for Todd to get out of the pool, but he ignored him and playfully dunked the girl under water and swam to the other side. Jonathan watched his every move and walked alongside the pool waiting for Todd to come out. Denise splashed water at him.

"Come on in Jonathan, it's nice in here," she said. He brushed her off without an answer and rushed over as Todd pulled himself up out of the pool.

"What the hell are you doing Todd? You're supposed to be watching my back?" Jonathan said while looking around suspiciously.

"Watching your back from what? Everybody's having a good time except you."

"Guys, come in the water," Sarah yelled.

"Yeah, we'll be right there girls," answered Todd.

"Listen, I'm not getting in the water, and now I'm really ready to leave. You're starting to piss me off."

"Alright, just chill for a minute, let me go change clothes."

"You got five minutes; then I leave without you."

As Todd went to change his clothes, Jonathan walked over to the food table where there was everything from shrimp to steak, he began to pick from the display while watching the swimmers enjoy themselves. A co-worker walked by and offered his condolences.

"Hey, man, I heard what happen at work. I'm sorry about that."

"Thanks, Clarence, but I'll be OK."

"If you need anything, you got my number, just give me a call."

"I will." Jonathan backed up and leaned against the wall watching the locker room for Todd. Sarah and Denise ran over to him, dripping water, they grabbed him by his hands urging him to go into the pool, but he just smiled and held firm. Todd ran back over still in swimwear and pulled from his pocket yet another small bag, of what else ... 'goodies.' Jonathan grit his teeth and shook his head in disgust, but the women were pleasantly surprised.

"Hey, put that away, let me go ask Jeanine if it's OK first," Sarah said.

"Go ahead, we'll wait for you," Todd replied.

"I can't believe you Todd, you're such an asshole."

"You're telling me you don't want any of this, Jonathan?"

"What's the matter Jonathan?" Denise asked.

Todd said, pointing his finger at Jonathan, "He knows what the matter is. I'll ask again, you don't want any?

Jonathan didn't respond he looked at Todd shaking his head in disgust.

"That's what I thought." Jonathan glared at Todd.

Denise stroked Jonathan's face. "Come on, sweetie, hang out with us," she said, as Sarah walked back over swiftly.

"She said it's OK, we can smoke, she said to save her some."

"No problem." Todd lifted the bag in the air, showing he had more than enough to go around, and then the four walked back to the locker room and smoked. They also took pills; Jonathan's irritation of Todd began to subside. Denise helped him loosen up by throwing herself at him and kissing him. The four went back to the pool area, and the girls jumped in the water.

"Come on man, get changed so you can get in," Todd said.

"Nope, I just wanna chill. She's got beach chairs around the pool, I'm just gonna sit here and enjoy my high."

"You wanna beer or something?" Todd asked.

"Yeah, I guess."

"Alright, I'll get it for you. I'm glad you're feeling better, now maybe you'll stop with the paranoia."

"Shut up, Todd."

"I'm just saying we're here to have a good time, right?"

"Yeah whatever man, just go get the drink."

"OK, I'm going. Hey, Sarah, Denise, you girls want anything to drink."

"Just get us whatever you guys are having," Sarah said. Denise motioned to Jonathan to come closer to the pool. He got out of his chair and went over to her smiling.

"Yes?" he asked.

"Help me out," she said.

He reached down, grabbed her by the hand, and helped her up out of the water. They walked over and sat down on two lounge chairs and talked for an hour. The young woman made Jonathan's anxiousness go away. They laughed and joked with each other. He felt relaxed.

"Are you OK?" she asked with a smile.

"Yeah, I'm fine, just feeling the high right now."

"Yeah, me too. He's got some good shit."

"Yep, you can always count on Todd for that."

"What is he a part-time dealer?"

"No, he just likes to get high so he keeps a little stash on hand."

"What about you?"

"Well, me, once in a while, but not like him."

"So how long were you with the company?"

"It would've been seven years this January."

"Well again, I'm sorry you lost your job."

"Thank you," Todd arrived with the drinks.

"Here you go one beer for my man, vodka and cranberry for the ladies; hey Sarah, come on your drink is here."

"What were you and Brian talking about over there, Todd?" Jonathan asked.

"He's having a problem with one of his programs on his computer."

"What's he asking you for, everybody knows you couldn't find your way around a computer if you had a map," The women giggled.

"Hey, I know enough."

The four raised their glasses and said cheers, and the two women down their drinks and ran back into the pool. Todd followed them. They all called for Jonathan to jump in, so he got up and ran toward the pool as if he were going to jump in, but he stopped short just at the edge of it and laughed at his friends. Todd hopped out of the water. Jonathan ran back to his chair, but Todd grabbed hold of him.

"Hey Brian, I got him. Let's throw him in!" he shouted to his conspirator.

"No, come on Todd. I told you I wasn't going in." Brian ran over along with five other young men to help grab hold of Jonathan. He wrestled to get away; he collapsed to the floor trying to make it more difficult to be thrown in.

"Grab his feet Bri," Todd said. Jonathan began laughing. Todd grabbed his hands and the other friends grabbed him by the arms and legs and raised him up over their heads, he continued to put up a fight. The spectators cheered and applauded as they walked him to the edge of the pool.

"Just surrender, Jonathan its over for you, you're going in one way or the other," Todd said.

Jonathan relaxed and just stretched out, and with a smile on his face, he looked around at all of his friends laughing and cheering, approving of his being tossed into the water.... Suddenly he noticed Azraa'el, sitting in the corner with four other angelic beings, dressed in white–Jonathan's joy quickly turned to fear.

"OK, guys on the count of three, we toss him in," Todd said Jonathan screamed.

"NO TODD, HE'S HERE, THE ANGELS HERE, PUT ME DOWN, DON'T DO IT! They counted, "One, two ..."

"NO, TODD. HE'S HERE!"

"Three!"

They tossed him into the water awkwardly but not before cracking his head on the edge of the pool. The friends cheered loudly. Todd and Brian high fived each other and ran around the pool with their hands in the air like two champions. Denise swam over to Jonathan, laughing and trying to help him out of the water, but he hadn't come to the surface. She swam under water and saw Jonathan not moving, blood began to swirl in the pool. She popped up out of the water.

"Something's wrong! Something's wrong with Jonathan, he's not moving and he's bleeding. Help me get him out!"

Todd jumped in the pool along with Brian, they grabbed hold of their unconscious friend and pulled him to the surface, and they swam with him to the edge of the pool.

"Come on, buddy, say something to me, it's me Todd."

He had a deep gash in the back of his head and blood gushed from it, they pulled him out of the pool and laid him on his back. Sarah checked his pulse. "Someone call an ambulance!" she shouted. Todd grabbed a towel and put it under Jonathan's head trying to stop the bleeding, the small crowd became silent and concerned as they gathered around him.

"Jonathan, can you hear me? Sarah do you know CPR?" Todd asked nervously.

"Yes everyone, give me some room; tilt his head back Todd," she replied.

She tried to breathe life back into him, pushing down on his chest, but he was still unresponsive, and blood continued to gush from his head. Another towel was needed; the first one was soaked in blood because of Jonathan slamming his head on the edge of the pool. He had also cracked a bone in his neck. His heart slowed to one beat every five seconds.

Sarah called his name, "Jonathan, can you hear me?" She checked his breathing. "This isn't good; he's barely breathing."

"Keep trying Sarah, the ambulance is on its way, but keep trying; I can't lose my best friend!"

Seven minutes had gone by and still no response, some of the onlookers began to cry as they stood near the lifeless body. Then Azraa'el and his companions moved in closer and hovered over Jonathan.

"Todd, I'm not getting a pulse; it's there but just barely," Sarah said hopelessly, as Todd started to lose control.

"Oh shit, come on man. What did I do?" Sarah continued trying to revive him, but he would not respond, at the threshold of death and unconscious, Jonathan saw his entire life from the time he was born up until that moment; he saw everything he was ever a part of, in sixty seconds.

The blood kept gushing from the back of his head; Todd put his hands to his mouth. He couldn't believe what was happening. He pushed Sarah out of the way and beat on Jonathan's chest, screaming for him to fight and to start breathing again. Tears formed in his eyes as he looked around at everyone, wishing someone could do something more to save Jonathan. He calmed himself momentarily and tried CPR again.

Sarah shook her head knowing it was no use; she grabbed Todd by the arm to stop him. On his knees leaning over his friend, he cried out regretting his playful but costly action.

Azraa'el circled the small crowd, but he kept his attention on Todd and looked down on him with no sympathy, and with half a smile, nodded at him knowing he would have to live with this ordeal for many years to come. The blood stopped gushing from Jonathan's head and now poured slowly; his heartbeat even slower as he drifted from this realm; he took a deep breath ... and died at 1am.

Now in the spirit, Jonathan was confused as he stood and watched his friends huddling. He met eyes with Azraa'el and then turned and saw his dead body; he slowly circled it, looking at what used to be him from every angle. He got down on the floor next to his body, thoroughly investigating his former self. He took his hand and ran it over the face, and then he shoved the body with his hands. He jolted back and then quickly stood up and looked around at all of his friends and saw them crying, he saw their sadness and felt as they did, he looked at the angel and said to him, "That's me; I'm dead ... I'm really dead."

Azraa'el nodded his head in agreement. "You never thought it would be your best friend that would bring about your death, did you?"

Jonathan didn't respond to Azraa'el's question. He turned and moved closer to Todd and put his hand on his shoulder. Todd was distraught.

The medical technicians arrived and tried to revive Jonathan, but they already knew he was gone. It would be hours before they took Jonathan's body from the scene. Todd stayed there until they did, and so did Jonathan and the angels as well.

"Azraa'el, he didn't mean to do this. Can you ask God to forgive him."

"You can ask yourself." Instantly, they move to the next realm.

CHAPTER 20
LIFE AFTER DEATH

A fast death and an apparent short journey Johnathan arrives in heaven. He looks at what appears to be his physical body which now has a surreal glow. In aww of the surrounding brilliance Johnathan acclaims

"Wow, is this heaven? It's beautiful here."

"Yes, it is," Azraa'el replied. "It is also where I leave you Jonathan."

"Wait, so what do I do now?"

"Elevate my son," the angel said and then disappeared.

Jonathan watched as the angel's energy dissipated, and then he looked around and smiled at the beautiful scenery; the colors were magnified a thousand times, and he breathed deeply and inhaled the sweet smell of the spirit world. He walked for hours looking around, investigating every little crevasse as he walked alongside a lake, admiring the clearness of the water. Fish jumped out of it saying,

"Peace be unto you Jonathan, elevate." He looked surprised, and not knowing how to respond, he bowed in appreciation and respect to them. Jonathan had already begun to feel a change in his being; he stood still and closed his eyes as a cool breeze came down on him. He looked up and noticed the trees and the branches swinging in the breeze; each leaf was perfect. He noticed one out of the thousands had turned brown. It fell gently from its position and lay at his feet. After a few seconds, the leaf rejuvenated itself; at that moment, a gust of wind brought it back to its position on the tree, and it regained its color. As Jonathan admired the tree, he heard the voice of a woman, "As the leaf fell from grace then reclaimed its life, so should you, Jonathan."

He looked around, trying to find where the voice came from, but saw no one, he continued walking through the garden of paradise sipping water from springs and smelling the sweet scent of every flower imaginable. The garden then became a corridor; on the walls of the corridor were moving images of Jonathan's life, from his birth up to his death, a review of all he'd ever done or thought to do. He became joyful at the images that posed him in a good light, but he felt shame when the images showed him in a less than positive light. His conscious spoke to him reminding him, "All that is done in the dark will manifest in the light." At that point, Jonathan closed his eyes, stretched his arms out to the sides, and said, "Forgive me." The images disappeared, and the corridor became a garden again. He smiled and walked feeling protected and loved, he had no fears or concerns, and he began to dance around, and as he did, he thought, "If this is death, I wish it would've happen sooner."

Immediately, a man who looked exactly like him but older, appeared; Jonathan looked with amazement; the man put his hand on Jonathan's shoulder and warned, "The Most High has set a time for all things and no hastening will cause the event to come any sooner."

Jonathan looked confused but shook his head in agreement anyway and asked, "Who are you? You look like me, but you're not me."

The man answered, "I am you, I am what we will become should you wish to elevate, so continue this path and be faithful."

"But why do you look older? I don't wanna get older. I thought you don't age here."

"We are the age we wish to be, and how would you know what you want and don't want? You haven't walked our path yet."

Instantly, the man was gone. Jonathan wondered what the older self-meant, but he quickly put it out of his mind. He had reached the first stage of spirituality, acceptance of the physical death, which took more time than he could have imagined.

As he walked, he thought back on his last day on earth, and his thoughts were made manifest, so that he might watch all that took place, even up to the last second of that day. Jonathan watched his best friend try to save his life. His death had come like a flash, and he felt sorrow for Todd. After Jonathan's death, Todd was hospitalized for a mental break down—five years would pass before he would recover. Jonathan felt a need to communicate to his friend that he should not think about the incident anymore, that he loved him and that he should move on with his life. At that moment, an angel appeared and hovered over him. She had black skin with a gold aura. Her hair was silver and long. She wore jewels around her neck. And, she moved as he moved, and it was a comfort to his spirit. He looked up at her curiously and asked, "Who are you?"

"Peace and blessings to you, Jonathan. I am the spirit being Sahli, the virtuous one, and whenever I hear the sorrowful thoughts of any being, I present myself as a comfort to those that wish to communicate their feelings to the lower level. You being a new spirit are without the knowledge to accomplish this. I've heard your words and felt your sorrow; be assured Jonathan that in the coming days, Todd will sit with friends, and they will remember you. The words you thought to communicate to him in this realm will be spoken exactly as you have said them by a friend in that realm. The desires of a spiritual being are always granted in the spirit world, as long as it is for the benefit of the being of whatever level you're attempting to reach. But, you are far from being able to affect any realm; you must first grow in your own spirituality, so for now, I will assist you in this communication.

"How?" he asked.

"I will take you to the realm of the subconscious human mind and we will enter the mind of one of the people that use to know you. We will cause them to dream about you, and we will send your words into their subconscious. They will speak your words to Todd when they are gathered together, and as you have suggested to your friend that he should move on, be sure to use the same advice for yourself while you are here."

"So there's a realm for the subconscious, that's unbelievable?"

"There is a realm for everything ever created so that all things may be reviewed and all beings would know we are aware of their every intention."

"OK, I understand, may I ask you something?"

"Of course, my child, what is it?"

"How long have I been dead? It feels like only yesterday."

"You've been walking toward the Most High for seven human years, but only one day in the spirit world; this world is forever Jonathan, so don't be concerned with time here. Only the Creator can keep accurate count of the days of your journey, your only concern should be gravitating toward the Supreme Being."

"Seven years! So where have I been for seven years?"

"You have been between the physical realm and the spirit realm, the abode of contemplation and for learning to accept your physical death. A place for questions like why did I die? How did I die? Do you miss your physical self? Do you have anger for being dead? Will you continue to be angry? And, the most important question of all, Will you elevate? This is where both the soul and spirit live until these questions are answered."

"So, I guess I answered the questions, huh?"

"You did, and this is why you are here now, the path of the walking."

"But, why don't I have any recollection of that place if I was there, because all I remember is my last day on earth and Azraa'el immediately bringing me here?" he asked with a confuse look.

"This was not your first stop, it was only made to look that way by the soul collector; you didn't come willingly to accept your physical death. You carried with you much resentment on your way between the physical realm and the spirit realm, and so, the soul collector held back your spiritual ascension, and his decisions are not questioned, for he knows best who will progress and who will not."

"Sounds like I almost didn't make it."

"You chose to grow Jonathan, and this is the best thing for you, for all new spirits."

The angel said a prayer for Jonathan and blessed him. She gave him a wooden staff to walk with and it held the aroma of frankincense. She then levitated and became an orb of light, moved across the skies at blinding speed, and disappeared. Jonathan marveled at the angel's exhibition in flight, and then focused his attention on the staff. He ran his hands over it, it was so smooth and perfect, and it had the word elevate carved in it; Jonathan thought on the angels words and felt his spirit renewed.

He was happy to be in the spirit world, he no longer allowed himself to feel anger or depression for existing no longer in the physical world. Azraa'el had warned him to accept his physical death immediately, saying that this would make the transformation easy for him, but Jonathan had forgotten the words of the angel and so his progression was impeded.

As he continued his trek through the heavens, a multicolored bird flew toward him; it danced around the aqua blue sky; its color was overwhelming and its aura pulsating. Jonathan watched the bird with amusement. He extended his arm, and the animated creature landed in his palm and whistled a tune, which resonated through the perfectly groomed place. Then said the bird to Jonathan, "In order to live forever, you must elevate." Immediately the bird transformed itself into a star and shot across the sky.

CHAPTER 21
CHLDREN OF PARIDISE

J onathan continued exploring his new level of existence, drinking from flowing springs, tasting the fruits of paradise, and seeing clearly, what he was not able to see before. Although he'd been walking nonstop, he never became fatigued, and anytime he had a thought, his environment would reflect what was in his mind. If he thought about rain, suddenly it would begin to rain; if he thought of having a drink, a spring of whatever drink he thought of would gush from the ground, just feet from his grasp.

When he thought of this beautiful paradise, the flowers would bloom brighter; the green pastures became plusher; and his spirit would soar. Jonathan continued on, and he walked one-hundred miles and saw what appeared to be an amusement park, where young children of all nationalities enjoyed themselves. He slowly approached them with a smile on his face.

The children stopped and called out, "Jonathan, over here, come and play with us."

He smiled at them then walked over with the excitement of a child to meet the young beings, "Hi kids," he said.

"Hello Jonathan," They said in harmony.

"Hey, how do you guys know my name?"

"We're spirits Jonathan, we know all who enter this realm, we've been here forever and we have the gifts."

"What do you mean you've been here forever, how long have you been dead?"

Then one of the girls in the group step forward, "Don't be silly, Jonathan. We have never experienced death only those who have gone to the physical world experience death. We have never left this realm; we are the children of paradise."

Then one of the boys spoke, "We watched from a distance the trouble the physical realm can bring to human beings, and even to spirit beings, if they're not careful, so we decided to stay here and keep our spirituality. We sit closest to the Most High, even closer than some of the prophets."

They all interjected, one after the other, like a rehearsed routine, explaining their existence on the highest realm.

"As children we were able to resist the temptation of that realm and we were intelligent enough to know that the physical is only temporary. And so the Most High's first in command, the angel Miykael, helped us remain, and he called us the children of paradise."

Jonathan sat down in a lush, grassy field in front of the children and questioned them.

"When did you know you didn't want to go to the physical world?" Jonathan asked.

Then another child step forward to speak. "Before the Most High allows you to be a separate spirit being, all things live within the Supreme, and we see as the Supreme Being sees, we feel what the Supreme feels, and we know what the Supreme knows.

Before actual separation of the Most High, a choice is given to you to be a physical spiritual being or to remain an entirely spiritual being, and looking at the physical world and knowing the spirit world, for us, we loved being in the presence of our Creator, so the choice was easy."

"Wow, you kids are smart. I wish I had known better, I would be like you right now."

A young boy named Joshua stepped forward and led Jonathan. "Well Jonathan, you will never gain the spiritual knowledge we possess except that you'll become like a child, and, if you wish to be as we are, merely say so with a sincere heart, and it will be. But, let it be understood that you will start a new journey and your destiny will change.

Because you are from the physical world, and you did not remain childlike or pious in that realm, you will have to become that in order to be a child of paradise. Your lessons will be taught to you by one of us who exists in this realm, and we being completely free of guilt and sin would be your spiritual teachers."

"You mean you would be my master teacher."

"No, your master teacher is someone who lived in the physical realm and has in common those things, the experience of growing in spirituality after harming his or her spirit and injuring his or her soul while in the physical form. You reached adulthood before your death, so you are not able to be a child of paradise, but you can be a student of this realm and elevate here. We are guiltless, without sin or sinful thoughts, perfect souls, and our teaching will truly lift your spirit, should you choose to continue your spiritual journey. We would show you this world in a way that no other spiritual being could; not even your master teacher could show you the way we would show you, and you will elevate. The Most High is our father, and we do not fail our father in helping souls to elevate."

"Well, how would you show me better than the master teacher would?"

"Not better Jonathan, just different, and you would see this world how you were meant to see it, through the eyes of a child. Our spirituality has never been in question because we remained in the spirit, as possible physical beings, and no one in the heavens can claim that except the Most High and the four appointed guardians."

"Who are the guardians?"

"The angelic beings that the Most High called first, Miykael, Gibrael, Raphael, and of course the soul collector, Azraa'el."

"Oh, I got to know Azraa'el really well before I came here."

"Of course you did Jonathan. All physical beings have and all physical beings will."

"He didn't like me very much."

"The lord of souls doesn't like many things about the physical realm, especially those beings that carry a title."

They stared at Jonathan and Jonathan stared at them; he waited for them to explain themselves, but they waited for him to ask.

"What do you mean a title?"

"Although you are here in the spirit world and have entered paradise, you carry the title ... "Murderer.""

Jonathan looked terrified, and pain came over his face. He looked to run away, but his legs would not move. His environment became dark, and the brightness of paradise lost its beauty as the flowers withered and the plush greenery turned brown. He looked around in a panic, feeling he was no longer in heaven. He felt physical again, and his spirit could not support him, so he fell down on his knees and began to cry. The children felt his pain, and illuminated themselves with a green aura, shielding themselves from his grief. They moved closer and extended their hands to him in mercy but did not touch him; Jonathan lay in the field with his face pressed against the grass for two earth years, crying, torturing himself by reviewing the dreadful act in his mind. He became angry with himself, wishing he had never taken part in it, and with tears in his eyes and a trembling voice, he finally stood up and shouted, "PLEASE FORGIVE ME!"

Then the children moved toward him; they lowered their protective aura, grabbed hold of him, and supported him. The grass became green again; the flowers were revived; the darkness subsided; and his paradise was beautiful again. Jonathan still teary eyed, smiled and hugged the children. He asked for forgiveness again and was granted a new aura, immediately. He looked at his hands, they began to glow, and the glow surrounded his spirit. He thanked the children for showing him humility; he thanked the garden for accepting him again.

One of the children addressed him, "Now, Jonathan, you must continue on, so what is your decision? Will you become a student of paradise or will you forge ahead on your own path?"

"I don't know, I'm sure I haven't learned all that I need to know here. Is there anything left for me to do? I like it here and I think I can grow but I don't wanna miss out on anything if I continue on my own?"

"You will not miss anything, The Most High created the spiritual levels so that we would acquire true knowledge of ourselves, to know each level of existence, to know the inner workings of the Supreme builder of things, and above all, to love the source of all things.

If you decide to stay with us, you would change your destiny; your experience would be different from the one you will have on your own. We would walk a different path, but you would still end up knowing all you should and all you want to know by the end of your journey, no matter which way you travel."

"So, it really makes no difference then, right?"

"In the grand scheme of things, no, not at all; this is about you making a decision."

"I would love to be a student of paradise, but I'm eager to meet my master teacher, and I know at this point, I can't have it both ways ... so ... I think I'll continue on my own path."

"Good for you, Jonathan. Your decision is the best decision, and if you wish, we will accompany you on your travel to meet your master teacher."

"I would be honored to have you guys along."

"Then let us move on."

"Hey, before we go, do you guys know who my teacher will be?"

"All we will say is that all master teachers are spiritually adequate, although they were physical beings, they have worked diligently to correct their spiritual flaws. They have become well versed in the knowledge and inner workings of their spiritual plane, and, at some point, they elevate and become students of one of the Most High's first four."

Jonathan walked with the children for six earth years, and he learned many of their names being ten thousand of them in this children's paradise. He learned their likes and dislikes and he came to love them. As they traveled through paradise, the children would perform exercises of spirituality, showing off their gifts. Levitation, disappearing and reappearing, mind penetration, and moving objects with thoughts, these are some of the higher forms of spiritual power. He begged them to teach him these things, but once he decided to go his own path, they would not honor his request. His wantonness to learn was responded with an, "In due time, Jonathan, in due time."

They walked in flower-laden valleys, hiked the highest mountains, and Jonathan swam in the most beautiful lakes. He asked the children questions constantly, and they gave answers to all his thoughts and questions. He told them jokes and attempted to befuddle them with riddles, but they have the highest of intellect after the Most High and the great four, so no riddle was too hard for them. They continued playfully chasing one another around the realm, playing the games children play. As they walked, Jonathan continued with his inquiry of the children.

After traveling a great distance, the children became silent, and, simultaneously, they stop walking. Jonathan walked ahead, and for all his talking he didn't notice his friends had stop their movement. He walked a little ways more. He turned and saw them standing motionless. "Hey, guys, what's up, why'd you stop walking, what are you tired?" he said jokingly, "Joshua, what's wrong?"
The child pointed to a small hilltop off in the distance. It was illuminated in a bright orange color, yet a cloud hovered over it, and sparks shot out from it. A shofar sounded. Jonathan smiled excitedly.

"Is that it, is that where were going, is that where the master teacher is?"

Rebecca, one of the girls, answered him, "Yes Jonathan, your teacher is there and that is his or her place of dwelling, and the teacher is aware that we're close by."

"OK, so now what do we do?"

"No Jonathan, this is your decision; the question is, what will you do?"

"I want to go there."

"OK, as you wish."

Three of the spirits stood on his right and three stood on his left and they grabbed him by his arms, lifted him up, and flew toward the master teacher's dwelling. The children brought Jonathan a half mile within the vicinity of the teacher's dwelling, and said to Jonathan, "This is where we must leave you my friend. You are a short distance from your master and now you must go on from here; our assignment is complete, and it's up to you to elevate to the next level. If you remain humble and steadfast in your desire to learn, the master will teach you all that we did not, and we did not because you are not assigned to us, but now your master will show you how to become a more advanced spiritual being, so until we cross paths again, peace to you Jonathan."

As Jonathan's companions moved away from him, he waved good-bye and watched them until they were gone; then he turned and faced the direction of the master teacher's dwelling, which now came into full view.

CHAPTER 22
THE MASTER TEACHER

An amethyst castle sat on a mountain, turning 360 degrees constantly. As Jonathan moved closer, he realized those were not sparks shooting out from it but the reflection of the sun hitting it as it turned, and he thought to himself, "I want to be there." Instantly he stood at the castle's hundred-foot tall wooden doors. In front of the doors patrolled seven different four-footed creatures: the bear [brute force], the elephant [intellect], the lion [fierceness], the horse [servitude], the monkey [swiftness], the giraffe [ability], and the dog [undying loyalty], and they spoke with him; the elephant first, "We know why you are here Jonathan, but tell us what your main purpose is."

Jonathan looked confused, not remembering that Azraa'el had told him that he would be able to communicate with four-footed creatures. He paused for a few seconds, staring at the animals, then answered, "I wanna meet my master teacher."

The elephant came toward him. "The goal of all beings should be to return to the Creator and to have mercy and forgiveness showered upon us, always remember that, human."

Jonathan nodded in agreement, but he was still looking at the animals with curiosity. "Forgive me, I'm new here," Jonathan replied.

"Can I ask you a question?"

"Yes, of course," the dog said.

"You guys aren't my teachers, are you?"

"No Jonathan, we are not," the lion said.

"Then why are you here meeting me?"

"We are here because he likes us; he says we represent his character when he walked in the physical world."

"And who is he?" Jonathan asked.

They pointed to door of the castle. Jonathan open it and walked in, and to his surprise, he saw an even more beautiful paradise than the one he had existed in for the past six and a half years. Exotic birds flew over him; lakes with the clearest blue water in which to admire every small fish imaginable; waterfalls that blocked open passages; and small angelic beings no bigger than his hand flew around.

Animals from the earthly realm existed together in peace. Although he was indoors, he appeared to be outdoors. The landscape was magnificent and it had no limits. He walked around slowly admiring the environment. He moved toward a plateau, and there stood a set of gold columns surrounding a sapphire throne. He put forth his hand to touch it, and it moved away from him. He looked confused and wondered why and how this platform could move itself, and why it moved from him. He looked to the air and saw the small beings gliding through it, and when he extended his hand to them, two of them flew toward him and they stood on his shoulders.

He asked with a soft voice, "And your names are?"

"I'm Sarafina,"

"I am Linda, and you are Jonathan," they replied.

Yes, and I'm here to meet my master teacher."

"OK, then call on your teacher," they said speaking simultaneously.

"What do you mean?" he asked.

"Were you not with the children of paradise?"

"Yes I was."

"And did they not tell you your master's name?"

"I'm afraid not, do you know the name?" he asked.

"We do."

The angels spelled out the name with a white powdery mist coming from their fingers and it lingered in the atmosphere. "That is the master teacher's name, but it is for you to speak it with your tongue."

Jonathan sounded out the name, "Rud ... wann."

Then the small angels flew away and stood at the top of a cave opening, in anticipation of the appearance of the master teacher. The four-footed animals laid down at the sound of the master's name, and the birds hovered in midair. All movement became still and the dwelling became completely silent.

A voice was coming from an unknown place; Jonathan could not see who was speaking. He stood in the middle of the dwelling and turned himself, looking around to find the voice.

"Jonathan, I am here to help you grow; this is my dwelling, my paradise, my heaven, all that I have asked for has been given to me. I have nothing but joy here. This entire realm belongs to me. I am a willing teacher to any that walk this path, which is why I exist here, that is, until I meet one of the great four, but, for now, this is my paradise, which I gratefully accept, and here is where I am the master teacher."

The dwelling became thick with mist and clouds, and the birds flew again singing a song for their teacher. A great energy moved through the environment. The mist and clouds blinded Jonathan, and he could only hear the rumblings of the dwelling.

The teacher walked up quietly behind Jonathan, and he did not perceive the teacher standing next to him, even though he stood seven feet two inches in height. The teachers face was that of an Asian, and he looked to be a little more than fifty years in age. His hair, with a streak of gray, was pulled straight back, and it fell past his shoulders. His brow was thick, his eyes were dark and piercing, the hair on his face rounded his mouth and jaw, and his physical body resembled a man of war; he was extremely muscular. His shoulders were straight and broad, as if he could move mountains with them; he wore a gold robe cut short at the shoulders, and his arms were bare, but gold bangles adorned with rubies and diamonds wrapped around each wrist. Rudwaan was a magnificent being. He possessed the look of a thousand years of wisdom.

He presented himself to Jonathan and said, "I am Rudwaan, a master teacher, appointed to this realm by the one who taught me. My goal is to learn from the great four and to reconnect with the Shangdi [God]. I am knowledgeable in all spiritual aspects in this realm concerning the lesser beings, including man. I have existed here in this dwelling for many lifetimes, and that is because I am fulfilled spiritually for the time being, all the lower beings including man must pass through this level in order to elevate spiritually, and I have been given charge over all that walk this path. I lived in the physical world during the fourth century. In the land of Asia, I was a soldier for the great warrior Attila. I've killed many a man and conquered the land of others; I was a lover of war and reveled in the defeat of those who opposed us. But, early did I die at the hand of my enemy on the battlefield, and there is where I met the lord of souls. At that moment, he asked of me, "Will you elevate?" and I replied to him, "Although I am dead, I will be remembered as a great man so what more elevation do I need?"

He then titled me "Rudwaan the murderous barbarian, Rudwaan the ruthless." This offended me, and I sought to attack him. He removed himself in the blink of an eye, and he reappeared and caused me to move swiftly through the levels of the spirit world. He did not transport me to heaven but to a place with no warmth and no love. Darkness was not recognizable darkness, but it was what the Shangdi called the triple stage, and nothing could be seen except what Lord Azraa'el allowed me to see. He asked of me again, in the deep of the darkness, if I would elevate, and, in my ignorance, I cursed him and sought to find him in the darkness—what a fool I was.

He allowed me to remain a fool, he took leave of me but did not leave me alone, nor did he leave his legion to assist me, but he summoned those who hate the humans, the demon beings, the Jinn. They immediately stood before me, one hundred in number; they stood upright like men, yet they were half the size of a full man. Their faces were deformed. They had treachery in their eyes, and they smiled an evil grin. These who hated the humans that caused death, rape, kidnapping, and pillaging. They hate the humans because of the status given to them by the Shangdi, and they feel we are ungrateful and so are pleased to go against us. They are a beastly looking species; some of them had moist slimy skin, and some with bodies covered with hair, and they smelled worse than anything you could imagine. They attacked me and spit at me, and their spit burned my spirit. At first I welcomed their challenge, after all I was great in the art of war, but this was not your basic war, this was constant battle, constant attack, coming from every direction and they used the power of the spirit world which I knew nothing about to attack me. And they launched balls of fire at me, hurling powerful wind at me, knocking me from one realm to the next, and then they chased me into the realm of the arrogant nonbeliever to continue their assignment. Yes, I had become an assignment for the demon beings, and they were relentless.

I thought I loved war, no! These were designed and created for war, to torment those who think they are superior and do not wish to know the Shangdi. I was a fool, a plaything to them. My attempts to fight back were to their amusement, and they laughed at and taunted me, and they bit at me like the dog. In the spirit world, you should not feel the pain of the physical world, but I felt pain, fatigue overtook me. I suffered shortness of breath, and I was weary of these creatures, but they never tired of me. They made sport of me, wagering which one of them could cause me to forsake my eternal existence, and there is no rest from them; whatever irritation you felt in the physical world, they would see to it that you suffer it here also. Time has no measure here, but I felt all the days of their torture. After two-hundred earth years of this painful badgering, I cried out, "SHANGDI, HELP ME!" Instantly, as if he were standing by the whole time, Azraa'el appeared and asked as he did two-hundred years before, "Will you elevate?" I fell to my knees, raised my arms to him, and replied softly, "Yes I will elevate." He lifted me to my feet, comforted me in the warmth of his energy, and spoke softly yet with firmness, saying, "There is none greater than the Shangdi; the Supreme Being is all there is and all there will ever be."

I nodded in agreement, and before leaving me, he presented me to one who would guide me toward being a better spiritual being, and I have been elevating ever since,"

Jonathan looked at the teacher with compassion, "That Azraa'el is something isn't he? He came to me and spent a little more than a week with me before I died; it was no picnic, I can tell you that. But now I'm here teacher, so will you show me what I need to do? I wanna elevate. I'm willing to learn and do whatever it takes to get where I have to go."

"Of course, my son. This is why I am here; my mission is to guide those who seek the truth and who ultimately want to rejoin the ranks of the Great Spirit beings, because, in the end, our return is to the Great Master, the Shangdi.

As he said this, he levitated upward and spun around. Jonathan looked up in awe of his new teacher, pointed to him, and said, "There, that's what I wanna learn how to do, how do you do that, just lift up in the air like that?"

"Jonathan this is all very simple, think back when you were in the garden, when you walked alone deep in thought."

"Yes, I remember that."

"As you thought on something, whatever your thought was, it manifested itself, did it not?"

"Yes, it did.

"Even as you stood some distance from my dwelling, you said to yourself "I want to be there," and, no sooner than your words were spoken, you were at the door, were you not?"

"Yes, I was."

"Well then, visualize yourself walking on air, flying, levitating, think it and it will be; all manifestations start with a thought. It is how the One, brought forth many. The physical man can accomplish this also if he doesn't allow his mind to be clouded with nonsense, but most humans cannot concentrate and focus their attention on things of this nature, so they are stuck, bound to the physical realm."

"Well I'm ready Rudwaan, I'm ready."

"OK, then use your thought."

Jonathan saw himself moving through the air, he stretched his hands out in front of him and thought to himself, "flight," and immediately lifted off his feet.

"Whoa! This is great, so you mean I could go anywhere just by thinking of the place?"

"You may travel anywhere in the spirit world, but traveling to other dimensions requires much more training, permission must be granted to enter other levels. Transporting from one dimension to another means you must take up a cause for that world, a mission, an assignment. You will not be allowed to just walk into the next dimension, you must have control over your spiritual power, and, without this control, you could disrupt the order of things on that plane. Many spirit beings have traveled to other levels never to return to the spirit world for not having the control of their power. They have gone into other worlds and have frighten or driven insane the inhabitants of these dimensions, because the spirit being was an unknown energy that the inhabitants of that world could not explain. These spirit beings would cause environmental change, move immovable objects, appear in ghost form, speak, but only create inaudible noise. The spirit being was never able to communicate with them; they took their spirituality lightly and drew the wrath of the one the Shangdi called first. I and my people called him Micah, his spirit name is Miykael, and he has made those beings to exist on whatever levels they are on until they are able to somehow restore order where they have caused disruption, or remain there for eternity."

"I keep hearing about this Miykael. He must be a real big shot, but what it sounds like to me is, if you mess up here you get thrown out of heaven, and you can't come back?"

"You may come back my son, but only after repairing what you have damaged, if that is at all possible; remember, if you seek to enter these realms, you must have the knowledge to control your power. You must be disciplined and remember you are from another world and not interfere to the point of changing the system of that world. Some have gone to these levels and set themselves up as one to be worshiped, only to find they are alone when all the inhabitants of that world have been returned to the Most High. So venture as far as you like but be mindful of your spirituality, and above all, control your spiritual powers; they are a gift from the Shangdi. There are beings that are far superior to you, and they are not so eager to leave the realm of spirituality. So they become the watchers of those that have done so, and they will record all of your actions and report back to the four leaders any transgressions you make. Traveling to other levels should only occur when you have chosen a mission and you seek to assist in improving the condition of the inhabitants and the environment of that level. Otherwise, you might cause them to believe you are the Shangdi, and this is an unforgivable thing to the four leaders, and they would for certain leave you to wallow in misery. All levels will experience the physical death; in turn, all beings will return to the Shangdi after this death. So for those who think to make themselves a God on whatever level they are on, they will remain a spirit, they will exist alone, for at that time there is no more life on that level. So then, who will worship you, who will seek your guidance, who will express their devotion to you? No one, and nothing, and your Godship was for but a moment in that time, and now you will exist alone ... forever."

"I got it, Rudwaan control my powers, as soon I get some that is, and when traveling to other levels, don't set myself up as God; there's only one true God."

Rudwaan looked at Jonathan with a smile and replied, "A more true statement could not be said, now as far as transporting oneself from here to there with great speed, you need only to think of yourself as a star shooting across the sky. Focus your mind on being in motion and at the speed you wish to move, think it and it will be."

"Well, I wanna do what you do, the way you guys just appear out of nowhere anytime you want to, how do I do that?"

"We never just appear from nowhere. When we appear, it is always from the spiritual realm, and, once you have chosen your spiritual destiny, you will be much more focused on what or who you are assigned to help. When your help is needed, you will immediately know it, but, as for now, if you want to travel great distances, think for a moment to the place you want to be and go."

With his words, the master had traveled five miles instantly, leaving Jonathan in his place, but then he spoke in a low voice from a great distance, as if he were standing right in front of him. "Now join me, Jonathan, focus and use your thought."

Jonathan thought to be near his teacher, and, with great speed, he moved toward him and stood before the master smiling. "So while I was on earth, you're saying I could have done this?"

"Yes, with extreme concentration and great focus, there are human beings accomplishing many acts of spirituality; levitation is but the simplest form of it."

"How do I become better at controlling my power?" Jonathan asked.

"Always acknowledge the Shangdi before doing anything, for this is all a gift from our beloved Creator, and then practice the gifts you become blessed with, use your insight. Practice staring into your mind's eye, all the while remembering that you aspire to become a better spirit being. Harness the mind, so that your ability to focus becomes as simple as the clap of your hands; in this way you can manifest many things here, and on other levels, even into other dimensions. Again dimension travel is something you should be well trained in and only the great four can bestow such training," Jonathan nodded in agreement.

"I thought you would know how to do that," Jonathan said.

"I am capable but I don't trust that I would be in full control of my powers to attempt it alone, I have great patience and I will wait for one of the four to fully assist me on dimension travel."

"OK, I understand. You know Azraa'el at times spoke to me through my mind. How was he able to do that."

"In order to accomplish this, you must first study the realm of the subconscious and learn the ways of the mind of all living beings. After mastering all the levels of the mental, you must go and live among each being in order to get the full understanding of that species. Mind penetration is one of the highest forms of spiritual power; again, that ability should be well mastered and understood before being attempted. Without superior strength and knowledge of this gift, you could cause great harm to the recipients of that realm, the great four are the scientist of this art; it was a blessing the Shangdi bestowed upon them when power over all the realms of existence was given to them. They pass this knowledge on to whoever seeks it with diligence in moving on in spirituality, and they are the best at determining who will elevate and who will not.

"Man, I feel like I'm back in school. It seems so hard; it's a lot of work. You seemed to know a lot about this stuff," Jonathan said with disappointment

"My master teacher taught me the lessons on spirituality. Some of these steps would not have had to be taken, had you been a more spiritual person in the physical world. Besides, you have forever to learn spirituality, and learning will be easy for those who desire what the Shangdi has offered."

"OK Rudwaan, what do we do now? I wanna go somewhere. Let's fly to another planet, let's go meet some extra-terrestrials," the teacher laughed.

"Jonathan do you have any idea what an extra-terrestrial is, we are all beings created by the Shangdi to each other we are different but to the Shangdi we are all one creation."

"No way ... I'm no freaking alien. Hey, come on. Let's go do something, let's go spy on people still alive; take me to the subconscious realm. That must be some spooky stuff right? No, I know where we should go; take me to the hall; you know where they keep the records of everyone that ever lived."

"The place is called the akashic records, and, speaking of such, I must tell you ... your father will come soon."

Jonathan looked surprised. "What happen?"

"Be at ease my son. He will arrive because of his heart stopping while he rested; of course, you will meet him and comfort him, but you will not stay with him very long. He will want to gather with his parents and old acquaintances and this will be his desire for some time. He will agree to elevate, but his will be a much slower process. Your parents have lived balanced lives as in they have not caused great harm to their fellow man, except for the normal things that may cause pain, such as separating from one whom you no longer find desirable and the physical battles of youth, but anything more does not apply to them."

"If it's just my father, why are you talking about both of them?"

"One of the reasons your father's elevation will be slow is that he will wait for his life mate to arrive, your mother, but she will not come for some time, but, when she does come, they will exist here together and will walk their spiritual paths as one, as they did on the physical realm."

"So, she'll be alone there?" he said sadly.

"No, your sister has married and has a three-year-old daughter; she will take her family to live in the house of your parents to prevent your mother from feeling lonely. Have no concerns of your mother, Jonathan; she is in great spirits, and neither is her health anything to worry about. She is among her family, and this makes her happy; it also helps in keeping her mind strong, as to not go into deep thoughts over her losses."

"OK, so my mom is fine then?"

"I would not say it if it were not true."

"Alright, so when do I meet my dad?"

"He will come very soon; the time is approaching, but first we must leave this sanctuary and travel onward."

"But I like it here, I feel comforted here."

"I'm sure you've been told time and time again that this is not about what you like, this is about progression and elevation; now focus and remember why you are on this level, or do you wish to discontinue your journey here?"

Jonathan stood quiet and thought how great it would be to stay where he is and to wait for his father but thought better of it.

"No, we should keep going. I can always come back to see Dad."

"Now you are learning, my son. Heaven is forever, and to stagnate over a single matter in the spiritual world would be considered a waste. Now think quickness and speed, and we shall arrive in the twilight realm.

CHAPTER 23

THE TWILIGHT REALM

Jonathan and Rudwaan arrived in the realm of twilight, with its purple neon sky, spring breeze, blue ocean, palm trees, and orange sand laced with tiny precious gems that lay beneath their feet. Jonathan untied the staff he had around his back and used it to support him on the sinking surface. He looked in amazement at his surroundings. Rudwaan was also impressed by the magnificent scenery. The moon appeared to be close enough to reach out and touch it. Roses of colors never before seen existed here, blue, black, and green; they danced and pulsated as the breeze swept across the realm, leaving in the air the smell of myrrh. Rudwaan fell to his knees and forced Jonathan to his, and they gave thanks to the Most High for creating such beauty; they gave thanks for the trees, the ocean, and the flowers, for their vibrant appearance.

As they walked along the twilight realm, they indulged in the fruits and drink of their new existence. Jonathan felt his spiritual abilities increasing, and he practiced levitating as Rudwaan continued his mentoring.

"This place is great. Have you been here before Rudwaan?"

"Only in the meditative state Jonathan. My master teacher instilled in me the highest form of thought projection, so in that way I have seen all the realms accessible to one who is on a spiritual journey."

"So, I guess every level is better than the next, huh?" Jonathan said with a smile.

"In the eye of the beholder, it may seem so, but all levels will have their own distinct beauty, otherwise what would be the point in exploring them."

"Look at me Rudwaan, I'm getting the hang of this stuff. I can lift off at will now," he said as he levitated.

"Give thanks to the Shangdi and be respectful of your ability, harness the power, and remember this is all spiritual, not for your amusement."

The two spirits walked two earth years and came upon a man sitting curled up under a tree weeping. Jonathan with a disturbed look on his face, walked over, put his hand on the man's shoulder, and turned him toward him. Rudwaan stood suspiciously behind Jonathan. The man was handsome. He was close to Jonathan in age and of his race.

"What's the matter my friend, why are you crying?" Jonathan asked.

"Well I've been here for a while, and I seem to have lost my way, and I don't know how to get back on my path," the man said.

Rudwaan pulled Jonathan back away from the man and asked,

"I am Rudwaan a master teacher, and if you have been here for a while, then why have you not called upon your master teacher, surely your master is here to guide you." Jonathan helped the man to his feet, and the stranger bowed respectfully to Rudwaan.

"This is true Rudwaan, but I cannot remember my master teacher's name to call on him, and I have walked great distances looking for him. I've ascended to the air and spoken to the birds. I've gone into the water and asked the beings that live there how I may find my teacher, and all have said to merely call out his name and that he would appear. But, in my distress, my mind has wandered, and I cannot at all recall his name."

"My son, when all else fails, for certain the Shangdi never fails, so why have you not called on the great one to rescue you and set you back on your path?"

Jonathan interjected, "Rudwaan, take it easy on him. Can't you see he is lost and afraid? Why can't we take him with us?"

"Yes, please take me with you. I'm just trying to find my way back," the stranger begged.

"We are in the spirit realm. There is no reason for fear or weeping. I am against you traveling with us; your path is your own, and walking with us will not bring you to your destiny."

The man, looking sad and hopeless, replied, "I am a lost soul looking for help. Please master, allow me your mercy. It may be that during our travels, I will find my teacher and rediscover my path."

"It is not for me to show you mercy; there is only one who can bestow that blessing."

Jonathan looked upon his teacher, displeased and confused. "RUDWAAN! Just let him come with us. How many times does he have to beg you?" Jonathan demanded.

The man looked defeated by the master teacher's words, but Rudwaan had no sympathy for him; he glared at the suspicious man, turned away from him, and continued walking.

"It's OK. You can come with us," Jonathan said. "Hey, what's your name?"

"My name uh ... uh, my name is Silbi."

"Silbi, that's a pretty weird name." Jonathan smiled and comforted the new companion.

They traveled together for some time. Jonathan became fond of the man, and even Rudwaan laughed at the disparaging jokes he would make about himself.

They had walked this spiritual path for one earth year. Then one evening while enjoying a dinner of cooked fish, fruits, vegetables, and drink, Jonathan noticed the stars losing their brightness. The moon positioned itself at a quarter full, as the night sky started to fade and a sun appeared to be rising. The cool breeze slowed and the temperature on the realm climbed, and the heavenly aroma was replaced by the most unpleasant scent.

The men rose to their feet and looked around in wonderment; they watched as the environment quickly changed from a beautiful breezy evening to a bright sunny day with exhausting heat.

"What's going on Rudwaan, why is it getting so warm, ewe, what is that awful smell, it smells like rotting flesh?" Jonathan asked. As his spirit began to vibrate at a rapid speed, he became irritated.

"Aw man, no more breeze, no early evening horizon, what the heck is happening? I want the old climate back Rudwaan!"

"This is not my doing," Rudwaan replied, as the rising temperature seemed not to bother him.

"Well, it's too hot. What do we do now?" Jonathan asked while trying to fan himself.

"Let's get in the water," said Silbi. The two men ran toward the ocean, but the water retreated from them and stayed away from where they stood; it would not thrust upon the shore. Jonathan looked at Silbi, and the newcomer suggested they take shelter.

"The trees, let's go under the trees, there we can find shade from the heat."

They ran back toward Rudwaan, who remained unmoved by the sudden uncomfortable conditions. They picked one tree from the many and stood under it. They felt temporary relief then silbi leaned up against it, and the leaves began to fall from it; the branches fell from it; the tree turned white and died.

Silbi then began to transform such that the cover he used to present himself as a man began to fade away and his true self was revealed. He now stood eight feet in height, with broad shoulders. He had the face of a man, but it protruded, making him look more like a dog, a jackal. His teeth were fanged, and his mouth dripped with slime and saliva. He breathed heavily, wheezing, and his skin turn brown. Boils that leaked pus and blood covered his body, which was also covered in course hair. He licked himself to ease the pain of his tortured skin.

He screamed out in agony and slammed his fist against the tree that died from him leaning on it; he broke it in half and up rooted it in anger because it revealed his true nature. Jonathan looked horrified. Rudwaan had the look of one whose suspicions had been confirmed, and so he grabbed from Jonathan the staff he had been using to walk with. He swung it at the legs of the jackal man, knocking him off his feet and onto his back. He stood over the beast and shouted, "WHO ARE YOU?"

The jackal man rose to his feet; he sought to grab hold of Rudwaan and do him harm, but at that moment four beings appeared instantly. They had thick wooly hair and their skin was dark like midnight. Three of them were youthful and one was the obvious elder. They wore white jalabiyas, and around their necks were chains of gold with amulets attached to them. They also were giants, standing fifteen feet in height. Silbi cowered at the sight of them. One who acted as the leader of the four came toward Jonathan and Rudwaan and spoke.

"I am Haku, and these are my sons Bilal, Yasir, and Ibraheem. Peace and blessings to you. We are from the realm of those that watch, and we are called the Raqeeb. This jackal beast is a rebel; he calls himself Silbi, which is Iblis in reverse. He is one of the many sons of the leader of the rebels, who we call Shaytaan the rebellious one, and who you call Satan, the deceiver or devil. This jinni and those like him exist in various levels of the spirit world, looking to deceive all who walk the path, and their purpose is to gain forgiveness and entrance back into the highest planes of spirituality. But, for them, there is no such forgiveness; theirs is an everlasting exile for causing the rebellion of the righteous, and there foolish rebellion was directed at the Supreme Being, the almighty, as if there was even a possibility it would cause an effect. But Miykael stood up first to put them down, and since then, they conspire to return home, but for you, son of Iblis, today your existence will come to an end for good."

Jonathan looked surprised, horrified by the beastly looking Iblis. He stood behind Rudwaan for protection

"Wait, Haku, please show mercy to me. I am innocent of what you accuse me. It is my father whom you seek to take captive, it is he who caused the righteous to rebel not me."

"You are from your father's loins, and we see you as we see him. You are a deceiver, a trait passed to you from your untrustworthy parents. We see no distinction in you, although you had a choice to be of good character, you chose not to be."   The jackal man fell to his knees and said, "I beg of you, Haku, hear my words. As a child, I watched the dissent between my father and my Uncle Miykael escalate over time, but I have nothing to do with that battle. I heard the disagreement they have with one another, and this is what was said between Miykael and my father. Miykael said, 'Son of the morning star, our Creator is aware of your dissent , I urge you to turn away from your rebellion and obey our Lord. And Shaytaan said, 'And who are you to tell me what I should do, Miykael? You were created the same as I. You have no authority over me. Why does our father make us to bow to this created being? We are created from the greatness of our Lord's mind and made to look beautiful. But, this thing is made from all the debris of the universe, and for sure, he will be a disappointment to us all, yet I should show reverence to him? Understand, Miykael, I don't rebel against our Father, it is this mud man, made from black mud and soot, and the left behind particles of what our Creator made glorious, that I oppose.'

To this Miykael said, 'It is the decree of the Supreme Being that man will be the ruler of the lowest realm, and this new being will be taught how to hold himself as a representative of the All Powerful. And he will be an example to the other worlds born after his, and when our Creator makes a decision there is no questioning it.'

Shaytaan said, 'Well, I am questioning it, brother Miykael, and what are you to do of it? As I said before, you have no rule over me.'

Now as my father and uncle spoke their words, support grew for my father, and many who thought like him, began to stand with him. Uncle Miykael looked around and found no support for him; he was surrounded by three thousand of his brothers and sisters who opposed him. Miykael then took flight and sought counsel with our Heavenly Father; the Creator spoke with him, strengthened him, and taught him the tactics of how to deal with my father, the rebellious son. The Most High blessed Uncle Miykael with great power, and even better, he instilled in him supreme intelligence, and this was so that he would foresee events before they took place. And he could hear the mumblings of those who opposed him even if they were in another dimension, the almighty made Miykael invincible. And Miykael recruited ten thousand who would follow him, and he taught them as the Creator taught him, but gave the secrets to only a select few, and he kept close to him my other uncles, Gabriel, Raphael, and Azraa'el. These became the great four who went out first against the rebellious ones. Miykael became the ruler over all the others, rebel or righteous; he was the warring angel and should not have been challenged. And he made my father to fear him, and my father hid himself whenever Miykael was near. He became cowardly and jealous of Miykael, and I learned to hate Miykael for belittling my father among the other spirit beings. This humiliation lasted within my father for fifty-thousand years.

So one day, I counseled my father that he should remember how he was created, that he and Miykael are the same, and that he should regain his strength in spirit and walk proudly among his peers. I said to him, 'Lift your shoulders father and speak to those who feel as you do, and go out and battle Miykael,' this I said before knowing the great power the Most High had bestowed upon him.

We caused a great divide in heaven, those who will follow my father the great rebel, and those who will follow Miykael, the supreme warrior. After many eons, my father and I had trained five-thousand rebels, but after learning of Miykael's great power, many of them returned to righteousness, but only two hundred were willing to go to war against Miykael; he was truly feared. We all knew he held the secrets of war given to him by the Most High, and we hated the fact that our Creator Father lifted him to such a prominent position. So, we looked to take him down and disappoint the source of all life; what fools we were to think we could provoke the Supreme Being; no, we were ignored by the Most High and drew the wrath of Miykael and his righteous warriors, and so the battle commenced.

My father fought by using the craft that moved through the air, and he avoided Miykael at all cost, but looked to shoot light beams at his righteous followers. The hope was that they would retreat, but they had the All Powerful on their side, and if the Creator is with them, how could we be victorious. Miykael and his followers used all the secrets given to them by the Lord Creator, and they used the light beams. Our beams never reached their targets, but theirs landed with precision and destroyed the realm we all shared.

Miykael chased my father throughout the universe; he made it his personal mission to show the Creator his loyalty, and at the same time destroy the newly named Shaytaan. He came upon him, and the two brothers fought ferociously. Miykael bound my father with gold rope and flung him out of paradise. He then commanded his group to hunt down all of my father's rebels and put them out of paradise as well. The righteous warriors moved quickly in capturing us, and we were thrown out of our heavenly home and made to live on the most inhospitable planets, some of us over here, some of us over there. In time we were drawn to the realm of the ones the Most High gave status to [those in the physical realm], and there is where we gathered and regrouped. My father existed alone on one of these heat-scorched planets, still bound with the gold rope, which nothing could free him from, but he retrained himself to use his insight and he became aware of this new realm. He used his thoughts to transport himself near the sun of his imprisoned home, and he went a distance close enough where the sun melted the rope freeing him, and he immediately found his two-hundred-rebel exiled army in the place called terra [earth]. This was the place made for the one we called Kadmon [Adam], the Most High's created being. The Creator gave this being his own heaven, making him free to do with it as he pleased. The Most High taught Kadmon all the things he should know about this new realm.

Kadmon was the source of all my fathers' problems, and so my father gathered his two-hundred followers and spoke with us, saying, 'Although this creature, made from the blackest mud, and who could not compare to me in beauty, nor can he match my intellect, neither does he possess my strength, and my hatred for him is immeasurable, we should not seek to end his life, for this would only bring a more violent wrath from our Father and our relentless brother. They have cast us out of the heavens and made us bitter, so we will set upon this Kadmon and his generations, and we will teach them the ways of deception, war, murder, and thievery. We will be subtle in our advances toward him; he will be mindful of us because his knowledge about the two-hundred exiled children will come directly from the Creator. So, his downfall will take great patience, but for sure, he will fall, and we will take his seed and intermingle them with us, and they will become like us, and we will remove them from the sight of the

Supreme Being. Miykael's protection will not find them, and Kadmon will not know the difference between them, the righteous and us the rebels, and we will take their women and they will bear offspring to us, and for sure, we will outnumber the righteous. So, let us begin the destruction of Kadmon and his off spring, and the children of the exiled ones will devour them, all because my brother has devoted himself to them, and this he did for the pleasure of the life giver. So, if they wish to have us remain outcast from the sight of the Most High, then we will make this new realm a hell for this created being.'

This has been the plan Haku, since we were cast out from our creator father's sight, but the Most High knew of our plans and fifty-thousand righteous beings were sent to assist Kadmon, then called Adam, on the physical realm. These righteous beings came to give balance to this realm, for my father and his followers had multiplied with the seed of Adam, and began to abound in evil.

The Most High sent the righteous to reverse what my father taught the off spring of Adam, and to re-instill in them the true way of living. They taught those who had not been touched by the two-hundred fallen, spirituality, the science of their world, music, art, medicine, and literature, but most of all, they were taught how to be like their Creator, which was to be God on earth. So, you see, Haku, it was my father's pain and jealousy, his feelings of being replaced as the beautiful morning star and the first son, that caused his rebellion, and I was just a son standing with his father at the time.

I now renounce all that I took part in; I hide myself from the righteous beings of this realm and from my father's followers on that realm. I am hunted like a beast for death, when all I wish for is to be back in the bosom of my Creator that I may continue to live as a spirit being. There is no future with the rebels; I renounce even their leader, my father. Haku, will you please show me mercy and bring me before one of the great four that I may plead to them also, for mercy?"

Haku stood in front of the jackal man and answered, "NO!" He then commanded the tree to live again, and then commanded the branches that fell from the dead tree to live again. They were like vine rope, they wrapped themselves around the hands and feet of the jackal man, and he began to weep like a sorrowful child. He begged

Haku, while being trapped by the tree, to grant him respite and allow him to live among the righteous again, but Haku struck him with his fist, and replied, "HOW DARE YOU APPEAR IN THE REALM OF THOSE WHO ASPIRE TO PERFECT THEIR SOULS? THERE WILL BE NO RESPITE FOR YOU OR YOUR KIND!" He then slammed his fist down into the sand, and this created a spark. He blew his breath at the spark and the spark turned to flame. The flame attached itself to diamonds, rubies, and emeralds and they began to burn.

Haku struck the surface again with his fist, this time creating a one-mile-deep crater. He pulled from the head of the jackal man, a hand full of hair and tossed it in, this caused an inferno within the pit, and he motioned for his sons to cast Iblis into the hole. The three young men lifted the panicked beast over their heads and slammed him into the crater, and at that moment, an even larger flame shot up from the pit.

Haku spoke, "And now you exist nevermore." He kicked the sand and stones into the pit, and the weeping sounds of pain from the jackal man could be heard coming from the fiery hole as he screamed out in agony.

Haku filled and covered the crater, and the beast was heard no more. Immediately, the environment returned to its twilight; the trees were revived; the water thrust back upon the shore; the sun dissipated as the moon returned to full position; and the breeze returned.

Haku walked over to Jonathan and said, "What is in secret will be revealed; deception and falsehood cannot exist here; and this beast truly made you his believer. Were it not for your master, you would have brought him to your next level, and then he would have deceived himself into believing he was truly ascending. But, EL Malik [the king] and his appointed are aware of them, and the Raqeeb [watchers] live in every realm, so for them there is no place to hide except to confuse the new spirit by taking on different appearances. So continue on, Jonathan, and be forever mindful of your surroundings and the beings you encounter. We bid you both peace and blessings."

Haku and his sons turned and walked a few feet away from Jonathan and Azraa'el. They stopped, extended their arms straight out in front of them, levitated, and flew across the sky until they were out of sight.

"Wow, that was crazy. Looks like I still have a lot to learn huh? So, what are they gonna do with him?"

"That is the end of him; he will exist no more."

"How'd you know he wasn't supposed to be with us," Jonathan asked?"

"When we came upon him, he was in a fretful state, and you should have been aware at that point Jonathan, there is no reason for unhappiness here, and there is no reason to feel lost or to wander aimlessly. There is no reason to have fear, and if he could not recall his master teacher's name, then by all means, he need merely call on the Shangdi, and instantly assistance would have arrived. But, he would not call on the Shangdi, because he does not belong here, and his fear was of being caught by the watchers, and so his fate was as it was, when they showed up.

"I understand Rudwaan."

"Good my son, now we must continue."

"Where to?"

"Toward the spirits," Rudwaan answered.

CHAPTER 24
THE ILLUMINATED GODS

The two spirits transported themselves to a realm called illumination, a place where the spirit beings glow like bright stars, and they are those who have been tested by the great four and have overcome temptation by the rogue spirit beings during the great divide. They have been given this realm and the title the illuminated beings.

Here is where master teachers come for new instructions given by the illuminated spirit, for this is their work, to counsel those who have questions about their next level of elevation. Jonathan was not here for counsel, but he would receive insight.

They arrived in this place and saw a multitude of people and beings whose appearance was very strange to them. Jonathan was surprised, but it also brought a smile to his face. Some of them greeted the two new arrivals with words of peace, and called them by name.

Jonathan extended his hand to return the greeting. Rudwaan smiled and nodded to the inhabitants of the realm. The beautiful landscape went on for an immeasurable distance. It was a neatly trimmed, grassy field with potted flowers surrounding the edges. The air held a sweet-smelling fragrance; the sound of stringed musical instruments was heard; and powerful beings, men, women, children, and beast from the physical world, and creatures from other worlds attended. These beings came from every part of the spiritual realm and presented themselves to a host of illuminated masters.

The physical appearance of these illuminated masters was that of men and women with pure energy, pure light surrounding their bodies, their aura. They sat on gold-pillowed thrones, and large columns divided one master from the other. Each individual being would stand in front of one of the illuminated master, and the master would speak no more than three words to them, and send them away.

This was the process for instruction. Those that were present could populate a small planet, and it was essential to set those seeking initiation on their path, and those who were just passing through on theirs.

"Where are we Rudwaan, why so many spirits and who are those glowing florescent-looking men and women?"

"I have never met any one of them, but I have heard of them, I'm sure these are the illuminated ones," Rudwaan replied.

Jonathan walked toward the thrones and stood in front of the illuminated gods. He approached one and said,

"Hello, and peace to you, I'm Jonathan, and this is Rudwaan."

"I am Isaac, and I know who you are."

"Where are we? I feel like I'm at rock concert, so many people," Jonathan asked.

"This is the place of instruction. The seekers here are those who come to a crossroads in their spiritual path. The illuminated masters you see around the field are the givers of those instructions, and we speak only what is needed to be known.

"Why do you glow like that, Isaac?" Jonathan asked.

Isaac wore his hair tied in a knot and part of it fell down his back; he had olive skin tone along with his illumination. He looked boyish not yet a man, with a slim build, he stood less than six feet tall. His every movement was swift and streaking; to take your eyes off him would bewilder you as to his whereabouts.

Without answering his question, Isaac placed Jonathan's palms on his chest, and with this, he was brought to the scene of how the illuminated ones were created; he was also allowed to view the entire existence of Isaac.

Born the son of two illuminated beings, he was pure energy but he inherited his status. Isaac grew strong in his abilities, and he traveled other dimensions at will, but he did not enter these realms until his strength and knowledge of them were tested and approved by the great four. He entered the class of those that become exalted with training and studying with the highest spiritual beings. His spirit and aura are of the green light from among the legion of righteous beings called the seraphim, those who only do what the Most High commands them to do. The title prince of light was given to him because of his ability to go to and from without losing control of his spiritual powers.

When those who lure away the righteous spirits approached him, he triumphed over them, the fallen angels. Isaac carries many titles, instructor, spirit advisor, purist, and he is ever thankful to the Creator and master of all things, for appointing Gabriel the revealer as his master teacher. He carries his titles proudly and without arrogance, and he is the example for the traveling spirit wishing to attain enlightenment and elevation.

After Jonathan viewed Isaac's spiritual ascension, he removed Jonathan's hands from his chest, and as he did, Jonathan lost his energy, almost disappearing, but Isaac restored him immediately.

"Let us go now Jonathan. There is good news."

"Oh yeah, what's the good news?"

"Your father is here."

Jonathan stood still with a look of surprise on his face; he didn't precede until he let the thought of his father being in the spirit world sink in.

"Isaac, my father died."

"Yes I know I just told you that. Now let's go, we'll meet him."

Isaac hooked Jonathan's arms with his arms, and they left Rudwaan in the field of illuminated ones. Their spirits moved and they were at the path of the walking, the first level, once again.

CHAPTER 25

DAD

As they arrived on the first level, they came upon a small crowd of spirit people. The two young men stood in awe, for in the mist of this group was the lord of souls; he towered above them, and his light was brighter than that of any of the spirits there. At the sight of him, Isaac fell down on his knees, prostrated, and said, "Peace be upon you, Lord Azraa'el."

Jonathan quickly fell down also and spoke the same words of peace to the lord of souls, and Azraa'el said to them, "Peace be with you, now stand my sons."

Then a man from among the group stepped forward."

"Dad!"

"Hello, son. Well.. I'm here."

"It's great to see you, Dad!" he said with laughter

"It's good to see you too son, it's been fifteen years and you haven't aged a bit," his dad said jokingly.

"Wow, has it been that long?"

"Yeah, Jon, how come you don't know that?" His dad said with a confused look on his face.

"I haven't really picked up on how to track time yet because here, it's like one big continuous day. I don't know from day to day month to month or year to year."

"Doesn't really matter, I guess," His dad replied.

"No, it doesn't, considering all the other great stuff you're going to learn."

"Boy, it sure is beautiful here." His dad said.

"Oh yes, but you ain't seen nothing yet ... So, how's Mom?"

"Your mother is fine considering; she took good care of me in my last days, she's a strong woman, with my condition she never got frazzled, and she never seemed overwhelmed by it all, of course she felt sad at times but she would never cry in front of me. Sometimes I would hear her in the bathroom, she held it all in so that I wouldn't worry about her, Imagine that. Yeah, she put up a great front. I even felt stronger toward the end because of her strength in dealing with that whole situation. But I'll tell ya, it came fast, and I'm glad for that. Even though your mother was a great help, I didn't want her to be burdened for months at a time with me."

"So, what was it Dad, how'd you die?"

"Well, first I had the stroke, then what finally did me in was the massive coronary, too many steak and cheese sandwiches and not enough exercise ... do it to you every time."

"Yeah, we know how much you love your steak and cheese."

"It was weird though, I left my body and watched them try to keep me alive, I thought it was silly you know, I'm standing in the corner of the hospital room and after a few minutes go by I start yelling at the doctors. HEY IM DEAD, JUST LEAVE ME ALONE ALREADY! And then real fast my family members showed up."

"Oh, so that's who those people are over there"?

"Yeah, that's my father, whom you never met, and my grandfather, also whom you never met, and ..."

"Hey that's Uncle Floyd." Jonathan said with surprise.

"Yes son, that's your Uncle Floyd."

"Well how come they didn't meet me when I got here? I wanna go over and say hello and meet your father and grandfather!"

Isaac then reminded Jonathan, "This is not the proper time to meet your relatives, this is your father's spiritual path, and to interact with them now could change your destiny. You would surely want to remain with them, and although it is your right to do so, you should be aware that your path will change."

"And who are you, son?" Jonathan's father looked confused.

"I am what you would call a guide, his guide." Isaac stated laughingly.

"He's right Dad. I better wait for the right time; hey how's Jen, what's my baby sis up to."

"your sister's great; she's a legal secretary for some big law firm in Jersey; she's married now, nice kid, guy she met while she was attending college, name's Joseph, he's a manager for a department store. Hey, I'm a grandpa now too. Yep Jen has got a three-year-old boy, that kid was the apple of my eye, your mother and I spoiled him rotten. I'm gonna miss them, you know."

"I know Dad, believe me I know ... and Steph, how is she doing?"

"Sorry kid, the last time we seen or heard from her, was the night you came to the house and told us what you were going through, who knew huh?"

"Yeah, well ya gotta move on, right?"

"That's right son, you gotta move on, but as for me, I'm staying put, I can't move on without your mother, well I can but I don't want to, she's the love of my life. Hell, she's my first love and I want her here with me I'm gonna wait, and whatever path she chooses to take, I'll take it with her, it's my option to do that, right?"

"Yeah Dad, and I think it's great, and if that's what'll make you happy then that's all that matters."

"Then it's settled I wait for mom," Jonathan put his left hand on his dad's shoulder; they smiled and embraced each other.

"I'm gonna build her a rose garden; she likes roses."

"OK Dad, sounds good, and I'll come back when she arrives she'll be here in about four years."

"I thought you didn't know how to track time here?

"They told me."

"How will she die?"

"That they didn't tell me, and they won't Dad, so don't be concerned with it. When it happens they'll find you, they will." His dad gave a confirming nod.

"So, what'll you do until then son?"

"Just continue on my spiritual journey, learning and growing, the things I should have done when I was there, you know being here makes you see yourself for who you really are, and there's no getting around that. I was a screw up in life, but now I can fix those character flaws, and I've been doing that since I got here. It's been fun, exciting, and sometimes scary, but I'm growing spiritually, I'm happy to be so aware of everything. Sounds crazy, but this is true living." He stretched out his arms and said, "I can feel myself becoming more in tune with every experience, I thank God for that."

"Good for you son, it's gonna take me a little longer to get where you're at, but I'll get there."

"Of course you will Dad. Well, I think I better get going. You're gonna be alright here, you know you could come with me and then come back for Mom later."

"No. I'll be fine, gonna wait for your mother, besides I have company; they're here to help when I need it."

"OK, I'm gonna go now, but I'll come back to meet Mom with you, when she arrives."

"That'll be great." Jonathan and Isaac turned and faced Azraa'el. They prostrated and thanked the lord of souls for arranging the meeting; they stood up and walked ten feet from Jonathan's father.

"I love you Dad."

"I love ya too son." They said good-bye and then slowly disappeared.

Jonathan and Isaac arrived back in the realm of illuminated masters; they moved through the crowd and came upon Rudwaan, receiving instruction. Jonathan ran over and stood anxiously by and watched as the illuminated being whispered in Rudwaan's right ear, then in the left ear, and then back to his right.

Rudwaan bowed to the master and backed away. Jonathan jumped in front of the being to receive his instruction, but the illuminated one shook his head no, and waved Jonathan away. Jonathan walked away from the master looking disappointed. He then went over to Rudwaan and Isaac.

"Hey why didn't he talk to me?"

"There's no reason to talk to you," Rudwaan said.

"So what did he say to you?" Jonathan asked.

"The message was for me Jonathan, and I don't have to tell you what it was."

"Fine, if that's how you feel about it. I just wanna know why I didn't get instruction."

"Are you not walking your path, Jonathan?" Isaac asked.

"Yes I am."

"Then why do you need instruction?"

"Well, I'd like to know what's next."

"What's next is that you'll continue on with Rudwaan, and I will now bid you both peace as you continue on your journey."

"So, is that it, were done here, nothing else to see or do?" Jonathan asked.

"That is all, Jonathan; it is time to go forward."

"OK Isaac, I'm grateful to you for taking me to see my dad."

"Don't thank me, Jonathan; there is only one to be thankful to."

"How would you like to proceed, we can walk or project? Rudwaan asked.

"I wanna walk; I get to see a lot more by walking."

"As you wish." They bowed to Isaac, wished him peace, and left the realm of the illuminated masters.

CHAPTER 26

JOHNATHAN'S TESTAMENT

After the two companions left the realm of the illuminated beings, Jonathan began to reflect on his experiences in the spirit world, and Rudwaan probed him to speak.

"So Jonathan, how would you say your transition from the physical to the spirit has been?"

"There's no comparison, at first it was a little difficult to deal with, the strange environment the strange beings, it all took some serious adjusting but now that I've come to a better understanding of what life is supposed to be, I have to say, it's the greatest feeling I've ever felt. You can't call where we come from living; don't get me wrong, I'm glad I was born and got to experience that world, but this is heaven, this is what we wish for in the physical. Azraa'el told me before I died that words could not explain in full what paradise is like, and I couldn't agree with him more. If we in the physical world, knew what it was like here, we would be more mindful of God, we would care more about each other, we wouldn't have so many mean-spirited people in the world. Before I died, to me, the world felt like such a cold place, void of any spirituality, so I became a part of that; the afterlife just seemed inconceivable, people back there doing the most horrible things to each other and just going on like nothing, and it's like God doesn't exist at all. But, they're wrong, it's so easy to see these things now. I feel like a real jerk for living the life I lived; now I understand the Dali Lama, Mother Teresa, and Gandhi; they understood, they got what it was all about. It's a shamed that I had to die to realize what it means to be a spiritual being I'll do better, with the little bit that I've learned so far, only makes me want to grow more spiritually. Rudwaan nodded in agreement.

"May the Shangdi bless you, Jonathan; you are truly walking the path to spiritual progress."

"Hey, you said you were a great warrior, how about showing me some of your combat skills?"

Jonathan and Rudwaan walked and talked great distances, engaging in friendly combat with each other along the way, Jonathan always on the losing end of course. They entertained each other's questions about their physical life, probing one another for answers as to why they made the choices they made.

As they walked, Jonathan noticed a small light shining in the distance. He urged Rudwaan that they should go toward it; Rudwaan disagreed but went anyway. As they came within two miles of the light, they could see it was not a light but a fire coming from a dreary damp forest. Wildlife was apparent by sound but not by sight. Because of the trees that stood more than five-hundred-feet tall, no sun, moon, or starlight could be seen or felt there.

Jonathan looked at Rudwaan with curiosity; they approached the forest with caution and saw a man and a woman huddling next to the fire. They were pale and unkempt. The woman's hair, in oily, twisted braids fell down to her legs; her lips were blistering; and boils covered the lower half of her body. She had died a young woman at age twenty-six, but the forest added forty years to her appearance. His hair was matted and riddled with tiny insects, and he scratched his scalp to the point of bleeding. Hair also grew over his face, even up to his eyes, and mud covered his pale skin from never being able to wash; Lord Azraa'el forbad water to spring forth for them. Tortured by biting bugs, they swatted themselves to keep them away; they were dressed in the same blood stained clothes they wore as the day they died, and their teeth were rotted; their fingernails were over grown; they looked like hunger and smelled like dead carcass. They lived like wild scavengers, eating the discarded left over's the animals let fall from the trees. Many of the four-footed creatures lived in this forest, but they never harmed the couple, that was not their mission. The animals' purpose of living in the forest was to watch the couples every movement and to not allow them to climb the trees, for to live in the trees was better than living on the hard-cold surface. Their dwelling was dark and freezing cold, while opposite them, separated by a mere twenty feet, where Jonathan and Rudwaan stood, was a beautiful paradise.

Jonathan greeted them, "Hello."

"Yeah?" The man responded.

"Hi, I'm Jonathan."

"Well hello, Jonathan," the man replied with sarcasm, "Yeah we know who you are."

"How do you know me?"

"Don't worry about how we know."

"So can I ask why are you guys here?"

"What do you mean why are we here?"

"Yes, why are you living here in this dark ugly place, burning a fire?"

"We got a fire because it's freezing here; what are you some kind of idiot?"

"But it's not cold here; do you realize where you're at sir?"

"Do you hear this guy, honey? What are you stupid? It's freezing out here. You mean to tell me you're not cold?" The man asked.

"No not at all."

"Yeah, we'll it's been extremely cold since we got here, and I'm tired of this fucking place!"

"How'd you get here, and what's that demolished car doing here, a car in heaven?" Jonathan said with a confused look.

"We died in that car; there was an accident, and we just ended up here. Jeeze, what's with the third degree? You got any more stupid questions?"

"Well about being cold, I don't get it, how are you so cold?"

"WE'RE COLD GOD DAMIT, WHAT THE HELL DO YOU WANT ME TO TELL YA, WE'RE COLD, WE'VE BEEN COLD, IT'S ALWAYS COLD, IT'S JUST

FUCKING COLD!" Jonathan thought for a second with a confused look on his face.

"But you know you can leave here at any time don't you?"

"Hey, smart ass, I been here forty-two years and I think I know what I can and can't do alright."

"Well then why don't you just do it? I think you two just need to ask God for help."

"OH you do, do you? Well who the hell are you to tell us what we need to do, get a load of this guy honey," The woman stared at Jonathan with a tiresome disgusted look.

"Yeah, we should take advice from you right?"

The man moved close to Jonathan and looked him directly in the eyes.

"Yeah we know who you are; sure, you're Jonathan, the LYING MURDERING BASTARD. YOU GOT A LOT OF NERVE!"

Rudwaan quickly turned and walked away, but Jonathan remained there speechless. The man continued his tirade, giving a full account of Jonathan's crime, and, after a few minutes, Jonathan slowly backed up, turned, and walked away from the man and his wife.

The man became angrier. "HEY, WHERE ARE YOU GOING JONATHAN? COME HERE, GET OVER HERE, DONT LEAVE! COME HERE YOU JERK! JONATHAN YOU MURDERING BASTARD COME BACK HERE! HELP US!" The sound of the man's voice resonated throughout the forest, unnerving the inhabitants, and after Jonathan put some distance between him and the couple, he turned to face them and spoke softly.

"I am not that person any more, you should ask to be forgiven and elevate yourselves." He turned and left the couple in the forest. Jonathan caught up with Rudwaan.

"Wow someone is in serious need of anger management, huh, hey, why'd you leave me back there?"

"You spoke words of encouragement to help lift them out of their wretchedness, which they did not accept. I saw no reason to stay among the unwilling spirits, and it would take greater power than ours to remove the coldness of their spirit. On the physical realm, they lived happily a life of inconsideration to their fellow man, and thought only of themselves. Not so much the woman but he, from his childhood, was forced to make decisions alone, and fend for himself. His parents drenched in irresponsibility, led a life of nothing but intoxication and did not guide him or show him the love children need. He allowed the seed of resentment to sprout within him and carried it into young adulthood then into manhood. He found the woman also abandon by her loved ones living in the world without shelter, and she was the only one he did show consideration to, and so they went on together, he trusted no one and taught her to do the same.

Cheating, lying, and stealing was their rule of life, and, on some occasions, it was unnecessary, but this became there amusement, and they caused emotional pain to others in the same way it was caused to them. But, the disappointment of others is no excuse for malevolence, and of course, they died together, a painful death, taking the lives of a husband, wife, and a small child in an auto accident. They were shown their lives by the soul collector when they reached the spiritual realm and they have not repented nor have they felt ashamed, yet they believed they were right in their actions because of how they were left alone by their parents. So, Azraa'el placed the automobile they killed the family with, in that dreadful place to remind them of their crime, and now they exist in the cold forest, confused hungry and appearing worse off than a four-legged animal. Soon the time will come when the spirit beings will appear to them and ask them one final time; to elevate; I pray they choose to do so."

"How did he know who I was and about my past, a guy like that you just wanna crack him one good time."

"They are wretched spirits, nevertheless they are spirit beings and they carry some spiritual powers, but as for you, Jonathan, until you reach full elevation and one of the great four come and take you to the next stage, you may come into contact with those that know of your great crime, and they, at any time, will remind you of it."

"But, I don't like hearing that, it bothers me. You were a warrior, you've taken lives, how come he didn't yell at you?"

"It should bother you, Jonathan. I have been spoken to in that manner many times and I remember for two-hundred earth years. I remained insolent in the spirit world and suffered all of the two-hundred years. Secondly, this is your path, you wanted to enter the forest and you engaged the man, so you will excuse me if I don't console you for the harsh words you received. As long as you are now conscious of your wrong deed then you are on the path to total forgiveness, it's a small price to pay for the life you've taken."

"Oh, so now you're going to jump on the bandwagon too, but I guess you're right, I can handle it."

"OK, then let us go forward." The two men walked in complete silence for one earth year. Jonathan thought of his place in the spirit world, and he was grateful. He thought only to elevate, and at that moment, the spirit being Sahli appeared. She hovered over the two men; they welcomed her comfort and thanked her for her presence. She did not speak but she smiled and led the men, they broke their silence and walked with joy and the angel directed them to walk up a mountain. They reached the top of the mountain and came upon three men and three women who were wearing physicians clothing, and a man lay stretched out on a table before them as they performed medical procedures on him. Sahli directed Rudwaan and Jonathan to watch closely; they moved closer and she stopped them from interacting with the men and women but she allowed them to come within fifteen feet of the physicians. The physicians were haste in their work, and Sahli said to Jonathan, "Go forward five feet my son," And he moved with caution closer, when at that moment the physicians spread themselves apart, to allow Jonathan to see what they were doing. They looked at him and did not speak, they pointed in the direction of the man, and Jonathan saw that there was a man on the table and standing next to the man was a seven-year-old child, and the child looked down at the man with a comforting look, he smiled and said to the man.

"You're OK now, the great doctors have fixed you." The man nodded his head, smiled, closed his eyes, and rested there on the table, the boy stood there with him holding his hand.

"That little kid looks like me when I was his age," Jonathan said.

"As he should, Jonathan, he is sprung from your loins."

"Huh?"

"Yes, the product of you and the rebel angel, Arianna, who you fornicated with on the physical realm, in the place of intoxication and who my brothers the great four destroyed for her persistent violations. The boy is being taught the art of medicine, for when he takes his place in the physical world, he will be one or two things, the greatest physician of his time or the evilest physician of his time. Being a dual spirit, he can obtain and bring about good change to that world, or he can choose to be an adversary to righteousness and bring about great tragedy.

As of now, we have great hope for him, but for many existing here, is far less challenging than existing there. The physicians who taught him are responsible for all medical procedures; they can medically repair every being in existence and they teach this science to those who wish for it to be there mission on the physical realm.

Of course, every species is different, so different procedures for different species, but the boy will have knowledge of medical procedure for every species. Because while in spirit and without form, he did pledged his allegiance to the great four, after giving his oath to the supreme physician, the Creator. His life will be closely guarded by six invisible seraphim, and one who is the highest-level student in the class of righteous defenders. This defender will be sufficient to protect him on the physical realm, for he is taught by Miykael, the warring angel.

The boy will have the right of choice, as all beings, but his is a very different right. We in the spirit world will watch his every movement. In addition to the six seraphim plus one warring angel, a class of twenty-three Raqeeb will be assigned to watch him from the spirit world as well; overall, thirty spirit beings will stand to the front, back, and sides of him.

Ultimately, we will not allow him to abuse his knowledge to the point; he will bring about a new species to destroy the Most Highs already established beings on that realm. We warn of this because with his knowledge and with the help of the rebels, should he wish to abandon his obligation to the Creator, even still, all things will be possible for him.

If an attempt like that were merely imagined by the boy, all thirty would descend on him with the words of allegiance he professed in the spirit world before he took form. If he did not abandon those thoughts, permission would be sought to end his physical life; the objective is for him to remember his spirituality and bring greatness to the physical world, in the form of medicine. Jonathan was shocked, even in awe of the boy scientist.

"Can I speak to him; maybe I can give him some advice so that he'll remember to be a good person when he gets there?" Jonathan asked.

"No one except these that have instructed him in the science of medical procedures, the great four, and our Creator can interact with him at this point. He has a great destiny and no one will be allowed to even approach him until his transformation, which will take place in one earth year."

"What's his name?"

"His name is known only by the Creator and the great four." Jonathan stared at the boy, imagining what life would be like for the child, how he would interact with other children, what school would he go to, who would be his mother and father. Jonathan asked the angel if he could just speak his feelings to the boy.

"You may speak your words he will not hear you, but words are powerful and when sent out to the universe they can effect change."

"OK then here it goes. Little boy ... well, I'll just call you little John, don't be like me, son; life is better than what might appear on the surface. Be good to people, follow your heart, and be good to strangers as well as your friends and family. Remember that you're a spiritual being and that you're gonna have to come back here one day, and you want it to be on good terms not like how I came back. Always remember above all, God is watching, oh yeah so is Azraa'el," he said with a smile.

"Will he be successful? Jonathan asked.

"Should he choose to be, he will be, he will bring the cures for many diseases and hope for that world when he arrives as a doctor and scientist."

"Good luck, little John, I mean ... doctor."

Jonathan and Rudwaan walked down the mountain Jonathan, very much in deep thought, Rudwaan was also overwhelmed with thoughts of the child.

"Wow that's my son Rudwaan, it's unbelievable, he's special, they made him into some kind of genius a savior to the world. I just can't believe that he's my son; he came from me. It makes me proud; he's a good-looking kid too."

"Yes, he is very extraordinary Jonathan," Sahli said. She still hovered above the men, and looked down on Jonathan and said, "Jonathan, biologically the boy is your seed, but make no mistake, when we decompose his molecules for transformation into the physical world, he will not be your offspring, he will be the son of a man and woman perfectly suited for his mission in that life. You will not recognize him; he will not carry your genes; nothing about you will be in him when he arrives on the physical realm, and he is what he is now for existing in the spirit world. Know that he was extracted from the rebel angel in the embryonic stage, and at the command of the Most High; Gabriel was ordered to nurture the embryo along with the great physician Ninti. She is the one responsible for the care of cells, DNA, and physical make up of human beings. As for your connection to the boy, this is not how you should think of him, for you will not interact with the child during his time on the physical realm. You will not be allowed to communicate your thoughts to him subconsciously, subliminally or while he is in deep sleep. This is a warning to you, any attempt to make contact with him while he is in the physical world, will bring great consequence. You will be seen as a rebel, and your spiritual existence will end. Do not be saddened by this decision Jonathan, during your spiritual elevation you may attend the akashic records and view his life as often as you please. But I suggest that you not become consumed with the progress of the child, to watch him constantly will not benefit you, it would only cause you to stagnate, and remember elevation is your goal,"

Jonathan absorbed the words of the spirit being and complied. "I understand his mission, and I won't try to contact him, but I will go to the hall of knowledge and look in on him from time to time. I still think it's great that he comes from me and that's how I'll always see it."

The angel looked down on Jonathan and smiled, pleased that he was not in a rebellious state and that he could see an important event coming to humankind and would not attempt to disrupt it.

The men continued walking, Jonathan still exuberant about the child, he and Rudwaan posed every question they could think of to the spirit being about the boy, suddenly she came down to the surface. Jonathan and Rudwaan looked at each other with curiosity the angel had never been within reach of them, always above them and now she is on the surface.

Jonathan asked, "Lord Sahli, why are you on the surface with us."

She did not respond; she walked around in a circle, stretched out her arms feeling the atmosphere, and then turned and faced the two men and said, "Fall down and prostrate yourselves." The men immediately fell to their knees and lay prostrate on the surface, and then came the sound of thunder and lightning roaring through the charged realm. The surface rumbled, the birds of paradise halted their flight and hovered in midair, those that live in the ocean thrust themselves upon the shore, branches of the trees swung violently. The hour of day constantly shifted, it went from morning to evening in seconds the wind was strong, and it rained heavily as the sun also shine brightly, mists from the ocean rush the shore, as if it were summoned to come forth. The four-legged beast moved to the area with cautious steps, the loin the elephant the bear the dog the crocs the serpent, beings from other realms and those from other worlds arrived and laid prostrate.

All in attendance showed reverence and humility, and out of the erratic atmosphere, a man appeared. He sat on a fiery red horse, and on his head was a crown adorned with four diamonds. He wore what many in the spirit world wrap themselves in, the jalabiya, and his was green, and on his feet he wore sandy brown boots that laced up to his calves.

His skin shined like polished gold; his face was gentle. He had jet-black hair, neatly cut; piercing brown eyes; and neatly trimmed facial hair was thick and silver and it fell down past his neck. Across his chest and under his arms, were thin bright gold leaves. He smiled at the multitude and raised from his side a great bull's horn. He sounded it and a great gust of wind carried the noise it blasted and went out through the entire realm. The angel Sahli bowed to him and she announced him saying,

"This is the great musician, the sounder of the alarm, the caller of the event, the great noise maker, and he who hurt the ears of the rebels who thought to devise a plan, and many of them went deaf at the sound of his shofar. He is the instrument maker, designer of the music, chords, notes, melodies, and rhythms. He creates the frequency that destroys buildings and mountains and can cause paralysis; he is the king of sound. Said the Creator to him, this is the third of the fourth, and this is the son of the All Powerful, the great Raphael."

At the sound of his name, he stood atop his horse and blew again his shofar, and another man appeared. His aura pulsated. He was eighteen feet in height, with a slender build. His skin tone was also golden and he shined brightly. His dark, bushy eyebrows and dark eyes gave contrast to his golden image.

His hair was black and cropped, and a crown with a sacred name emblazoned on the front of it sat on his head. Gold rings adorned his fingers. He held a large silver book, which stood five feet in height and four feet across, with a gold and black ribbon tied around it. This was the book of the new message, with new teachings from the Most High to the men of the new age forthcoming.

He too wore a green jalabiya, and it covered him from his shoulder to the length of his feet. He stood in their presence smiling, and at his arrival, off in the distance from the east, a legion of seven-thousand spirit beings. These came from every nationality, and stood on the waters humming a melody in honor of him, and he acknowledge the spirits and lifted his arm and waved it over the multitude of created beings, and instantly every prophet, messenger, and fighter of evil stood next to him.

The angel Sahli bowed to him and she announced him saying, "This is the revealer, the one who listened and did not speak as the Most High taught him. He is the book writer, the prophet teacher, the great instructor, the proof of the Most High, the carrier of the holy messages, protector of the writings, the second witness, the second warrior, the bender of the knees of all beings, the time traveler, the principle, the one who proves without a shadow of a doubt, the teacher of those who search for the Supreme Being, the bringer of the word of God, the second in command, the son of the All Powerful, the great Gibrael."

The multitude gazed upon him with reverence and awe, and he lifted himself off the surface and spoke to the created beings; his voice went out through the realm, causing all present to vibrate and levitate, and he said, "I am Gibrael, and you find me to be exalted, but even I am a created being, and I am nothing next to the one that produced me. There is only one that is truly exalted above all."

The multitude cried tears of joy at the thought of this great being addressing them with words and blessing them to look upon all the great messengers and prophets from history.

Gibrael settled the multitude as he levitated himself higher, and with that, more beings from every level entered the realm to gaze upon the commanding angels. Suddenly one-hundred-thousand spirit beings appeared all wearing white jalabiyas; they appeared as men, women, and children from all races.

They carried gifts for the highest angels; some carried flowers; some carried gold; and some carried fragrant sticks. They sang the praises of our Creator. Then Gibrael waved his hand and extended this paradise making the realm even more spacious, and the multitude cheered his ability.

Raphael blew his shofar for a third time, and the sky lit up with a rainbow gracing the nightly realm; springs of drink appeared; and the aroma of the heaven became even sweeter. The spirits of the multitude were raised, and they rejoiced and were grateful. Then two-hundred-thousand visitors were witnessing the spirit realm and the power of the angelic beings. A soft voice was heard resonating through the realm repeating the words, "Peace and blessing, peace and blessing, blessed are you for choosing elevation, peace and blessings, peace and blessings." The words were like a song to the multitude, which looked around with joy and anticipation of who was sending the blessing, but the voice came from every direction, and it continued for one hour, and the multitude became excited, and they began to sing the words and dance to the song of the unidentifiable voice.

All of heaven heard the singing and dancing, and the multitude congratulated each other, knowing that all that were there were meant to be there, and that they would be moving forward and acquiring new spiritual abilities, moving on to higher levels in the spirit world. As the multitude received the telepathic news, in their excitement, they were unaware of him coming down from his position.

In the heavens, his dwelling is near to the Most High. He opened the sky and drifted unseen to the multitude, until he came down and was in the midst of the occupants. Then only the two great angels could see him; Raphael sounded his shofar once again and stilled the multitude. They looked upon the noisemaker with wondering. His noise was the loudest they had heard, and he made the sound last. As the shofar was sounding, Gibrael lifted his arm, drew an invisible line, and divided the multitude into two sections evenly, and a valley was left between them, and then he that came down gradually materialized, making himself visible to the multitude.

They stopped their movements, being struck with awe, surprise, and confusion, for they could not comprehend what they were witnessing, their eyes fixed on him. He appeared as a five-year-old child, with jet-black hair, light-brown eyes, and caramel skin, and he wore a white shirt with a green sash around the waist, with sleeves just past his elbows; pants that matched his shirt; and sandals on his feet. He stood atop a golden chariot like those of ancient times, holding in his hands chains made of gold. The chains were attached to one hundred disgraced fallen angels, whom he turned into demons, and they pulled his chariot through the valley between the multitudes. The multitude stared at this one as he stepped down from his chariot and walked out in front of the demons, which with humility looked upon him and spoke. "Please forgive us lord, and have mercy on us, allow us back into this beautiful realm."

The young boy looked sternly at the demons and asked with the voice of a child, "Where is your leader now, the rebel, the one we cast down, the one who foolishly conspired to take control of the heavens, the one who became jealous of the new being, the one who hated me and rebelled against our Creator? No, your existence will now come to an end."

The young boy raised his arms above his head and clapped his hands together, and the one-hundred demons were immediately blown to pieces and incinerated.

The multitude cowered in fear, as the young boy slowly began to grow in height, towering even over the trees, and as he grew, he morphed, displaying himself as a warrior god from every age of man's existence, posing first with the sling shot, then as a muscle-bound man with the spiked club, then with a bow and arrow, then a sword and shield, then with a gun, and then a laser gun, until finally, he threw down his weapons then raised his hands into the air and brought down the rain. Next, he brought the sun close to the realm and stopped the rain. Then Sahli rushed toward him, bowed to him, and made known exactly who he was. "This is the great defender, the warring angel, the ancient of days, the expeller of the rebels, the first to do battle without being commanded, the possessor of the high sciences, the prince of spirits, the older brother, the dimension traveler, the metamorphoses, the one who stands alone, the witness to all things done by the Creator, the capable one, the righteous warrior, the one who defeats those who challenge him, the one whom God gave no limits, the first to be called, the first to come forward, the most knowledgeable after the Most High, the one with the most humility in the presence of the Most High, the benefactor of the Most High, the best teacher after the Most High, the one most devoted to the Most High, the one who is most like the Most High, he is Miykael, the archangel. This is the son of the Most High, this is Michael the great."

After the introduction, all who were present stood up to gaze upon the first in command. Jonathan and Rudwaan slowly rose to their feet. Rudwaan, with tears in his eyes, could only stare at this great spirit being with total admiration and love. He knew of him and knew of his greatness, and could not understand why such a being of his honor would appear to them. Jonathan with complete humility extended his hand and attempted to approach the most powerful of all the angels, but Sahli spoke and said to Jonathan, "Hold yourself back Jonathan, the presence of our brother is for a reason. He is here that you might see greatness, power, and humility, next to the Supreme Being, there is none higher than him, and you should not approach him unless he gives permission."

Miykael smiled warmly at the gathered spirit being and extended his hand to Jonathan. Jonathan grabbed it and felt a warm sensation, and, in his mind, he saw the history of this grand angelic being, and he bowed on one knee to him and heard the words reaching every realm in the spirit world come from Miykael saying, "I am known by many names, but most know me as Miykael or Michael. I am your brother and your father, because in the eyes of the omnipresent soul, I am above you. Your admiration of me is understood, but I am nothing compared to the one who brought forth all life and is the re-caller of all events. So magnificent is the great designer, to attempt to give a description would be a sin, for not even my words can complement the All Powerful one. When you look upon me, bring to mind that I am what I am by way of the one who bestowed blessings on me. I am not a creation of myself but of the one who created all beings. First, the self, then from one came two, from two came four, and from four came eight, we continued, and by command of the great scientist, we multiplied. I am the defender of the Supreme Creator, not because our Lord is in need of defending but because I enjoy defending our Creator from blasphemous words or thoughts of those who should show gratitude. And all that I possess in power are blessing from the Most High, but if the Most High thought to destroy you or I, or any created being, nothing could prevent it, and the mere thought from the great soul would bring about a manifestation, and nothing can prevent it. And you my children should never cease to give thanks to the one who spoke words, and made everything come into existence, and then you would begin to know your Creator."

The great angel gazed into Jonathan's eyes and responded to his thoughts saying, "I am not here for you today, my son, but it is your friend and teacher Rudwaan that I must take away." He then pulled out of the air, a gold crown and asked the overwhelmed warrior, "Now what will be your mission, Rudwaan?"

Rudwaan lowered his eyes and with tears, heavy breathing and in humility replied, "To learn from you Lord Micah, for with you my elevation is certain."

Miykael then placed the crown on Rudwaan's head. "You have had many souls come to you for guidance, and you have taught them what was taught to you, and now for your service to these wandering spirits, you will follow me, and I will teach you one of the sciences given to me by the Creator. In your thoughts, you ask why is it that you will be taught only one science, and I say to you, to possess knowledge of even one of the great sciences will raise you from a master teacher to a supreme teacher. There will be no restrictions on you as to how you use whatever science you wish to learn, as long as your thoughts are for the benefit of the universe. And with this crown all in the spirit world will recognize you as a student of one the great four master teachers."

Rudwaan feeling very humbled, cried and smiled at the same time and replied.

"I am sure I am not worthy of your blessing, my Lord, but I will accept it any way."

Rudwaan smiled and embraced the great angel and he too saw the history of Miykael and became even more in awe of him. From the seven-thousand angels that stood in the distance, twelve immediately appeared on the land and surrounded Rudwaan; they encouraged him and made him their brother, and prepared to take him away.

Miykael then spoke with Jonathan, "We must leave you now, for this will be a time for continued elevation of the soul and spirit. You have learned from one of the best master teachers. I say to you all, remember the Most High in all endeavors great and small and you will move quickly to the ultimate goal, the meeting with the creator of all things"

Rudwaan stood among his new family of spirit beings, and overwhelmed with joy he shouted to Jonathan, "Elevate Jonathan!" The seven-thousand spirit beings looked to their leader for instruction. Miykael nodded his head, and the twelve spirits held Rudwaan by the hand and collectively dissipated their energy and took him away. Jonathan looked on waving good-bye as they faded into the atmosphere. Then Miykael the great stood before him, smiling, he waved his hand over his body and became pure light. The light was immense and it vibrated with sound and became many colors, it levitated and circled the multitude, and then immediately they traveled a great distance in the blink of an eye and the great angel was seen no more. Alone now, Jonathan cried like a child, overwhelmed by the presence of the Great Spirit beings, he looked to Sahli for his instruction.

She levitated back to the air, and then looked down on him smiling saying, "You must continue on, Jonathan."

"Wow ... Why couldn't I go with them? That would have been so cool," he said as he wiped tears from his eyes.

"Miykael is awesome. He is so powerful. Rudwaan is one of them now. He is going to learn from him. Unbelievable!" Sahli responded.

"To be taught by one of the great four is certainly an honor and is something you should strive for. They are the closest to the Creator that you will see until your personal meeting with the Most High. Yet you should consider that Rudwaan existed here for some time and although he had even been obstinate for a while, ultimately, he was forced to see the true way to spirituality. Your experience is very different. You did not have to be forced, and the great Azraa'el even visited with you before you arrived, and he prepared you for some of the things you should know about the afterlife. If you remember that you are working to raise your spirituality, to reconnect to the Supreme Being, you too will also be chosen to be a student of the wise ones."

"I'll remember and I'll stay focused. I'm so inspired by what just happen here; it means I can be like them, I can be a real spiritual being and be powerful. Yes, I want that."

Jonathan continued to walk in the shadow hour of the realm, very happy knowing that he could be called, as Rudwaan was, to learn from one of the four. He walked with renewed energy, jumping great heights into trees, levitating, running at remarkable speeds, he elevated his abilities a thousand times more. He peeked into other realms using his mind, practicing movement by thought; these sciences he would master only by being taught by one of the great four. Jonathan walked with the angel Sahli for one earth year. Then, in his seventeenth year in the spirit world, she also left him. "Know that when I'm needed by you, I will immediately appear. You are doing well, and I must go, for there are new arrivals that are in distress about their new world. Move forward, my son, elevation."

She spread her arms and flew like A bird with wings, she moved with the wind and became transparent he watched until he could see her no more. He continued his joyful exuberance, basking in the news that one day he would be joining the class of those who learn from the great teachers, and, more importantly, Jonathan felt he acquired new friendships and new family. He appreciated the spirit world even more than before, and he moved through the realm with comfort. This was his home, and he was happy to be here. He came upon a tree bearing fruit, he picked from it and sat under it and thought back on his long journey, even of his days in the physical world. He had no more guilt or sadness; he now began to understand truly that spirituality is all that the Most High wishes for the created beings.

Jonathan stood up and began walking again. He tried to still his mind of all thoughts, but now he had the music to his favorite song in his mind and at that thought to his surprise the music began to play loudly throughout his paradise. As his mind switched to a more somber mood, Jonathan inhaled the tranquility of heaven and wondered about his parents. His concerns were not as much for his father as they were for his mother. Then suddenly a bright light fell from above, striking the surface and causing a controlled fire. Out of the fire walked the lord of souls, Azraa'el, and Jonathan fell to his knees and praised the great being, and he spoke to him, "My lord, I feel my mother getting weak. I know she'll come here soon. I'm just not exactly sure when."

"Stand, my son, indeed she is in the waning stage of her life there, and you will know of her arrival when that time comes and not before."

"I understand. I just wanna meet her when she comes."

"You will."

"Can I ask you a question?"

"Of course, Jonathan."

"Why do all you angels look like human beings?"

"I would not say that we look like human beings. I would say you look like us. Now, look abroad my son."

Jonathan looked out over the night horizon and witnessed two orbs of light, one bigger and shining brighter than the other; they shifted up and down, and circled each other. They began moving toward him, and Jonathan stood still as he marveled at the two light forms. He wondered what they could be but could not bring himself to ask the angel. The beams of light perceived his thoughts; in a flash, they stood before him, and simultaneously the orbs gave their greeting.

"May the blessings of the Supreme Creator remain with you, Lord Azraa'el, and may peace be with you, Jonathan."

Azraa'el nodded, acknowledging them. Jonathan moved closer to inspect the light forms, but immediately they accelerated upward at an untraceable speed. They flew around erratically and then returned to the surface just as quickly. Then, they slowed down their vibration and gradually lowered their spiritual light and spoke again. "Hello Jonathan."

After the vibrancy of their aura dissipated, Jonathan looked harder at the two beings. His eyes widen as he recognized them. "Mikey? ... Jimmy? ... Holy sh–!"

www.ingramcontent.com/pod-product-compliance
Lightning Source LLC
Chambersburg PA
CBHW051823040426
42447CB00006B/333